CW01390933

The HERB Kitchen

The HERB Kitchen

RECIPES FOR ENJOYING & USING HERBS IN YOUR COOKING

rps

RYLAND PETERS & SMALL

Senior Designer Toni Kay
Senior Editor Abi Waters
Production Manager
Gordana Simakovic
Creative Director
Leslie Harrington
Editorial Director Julia Charles

Indexer Vanessa Bird

First published in 2025 by
Ryland Peters & Small
20–21 Jockey's Fields, London
WC1R 4BW
and
1452 Davis Bugg Road
Warrenton, NC 27589

www.rylandpeters.com
email: euregulations@rylandpeters.com

10 9 8 7 6 5 4 3 2 1

Text © Caroline Artiss, Julia Charles,
Megan Davies, Ursula Ferrigno, Nicola
Graimes, Tori Haschka, Kathy Kordalis,
Jenny Linford, Uyen Luu, Hannah Miles,
Orlando Murrin, Louise Pickford, Barbara
Segall and Ryland Peters & Small 2025
Design and commissioned photography
© Ryland Peters & Small 2025

Printed in China.

The author's moral rights have been
asserted. All rights reserved. No part of this
publication may be reproduced, stored in a
retrieval system or transmitted in any form
or by any means, electronic, mechanical,
photocopying or otherwise, without the
prior permission of the publisher.

ISBN: 978-1-78879-687-3

A CIP record for this book is available
from the British Library.
US Library of Congress cataloging-in-
Publication Data has been applied for.

The authorised representative in the EEA is
Authorised Rep Compliance Ltd.,
Ground Floor, 71 Lower Baggot Street,
Dublin, D02 P593, Ireland
www.arccompliance.com

NOTES
• All spoon measurements are level unless
otherwise specified.
• All herbs used are fresh unless otherwise
specified.
• All eggs are medium (UK) or large (US),
unless specified as large, in which case
US extra-large should be used. Uncooked
or partially cooked eggs should not
be served to the very old, frail, young
children, pregnant women or those with
compromised immune systems.
• When a recipe calls for cling film/plastic
wrap, you can substitute for beeswax wraps,
silicone stretch lids or compostable baking
paper for greater sustainability.
• When a recipe calls for the grated zest of
citrus fruit, buy unwaxed fruit and wash
well before using.
• Ovens should be preheated to the specified
temperatures. If using a fan-assisted oven,
adjust temperatures according to the
manufacturer's instructions.

FSC
www.fsc.org

MIX
Paper | Supporting
responsible forestry
FSC® C008047

Contents

Introduction 6

THE HERBS 8

Basil 10 • Bay 11

Chamomile 12 • Chervil 13

Chives & Garlic Chives, Coriander 14

Dill 16 • Fennel 17 • Garlic 18

Lavender 19 • Lemon Balm 20

Lovage 21 • Mint 22

Oregano or Marjoram 23

Parsley & Rosemary 24 • Sage 26

Sorrel 27 • Tarragon 28 • Thyme 29

How to Grow Herbs 30

SAUCES & DRESSINGS 34

SALADS, SOUPS & LIGHT
PLATES 46

MAIN DISHES 76

SWEET THINGS & DRINKS 108

Index 126

Credits 128

Introduction

Herbs have been valued for thousands of years for their aromatic and health-giving qualities as well as culinary uses. Today they bring a fresh pop of colour to any kitchen corner, add interest to window boxes or thrive as a sweet-smelling addition to any garden. From mint to marjoram, herbs are undoubtedly the easiest way to add instant vibrancy, interest and brightness to your everyday cooking.

This fresh collection of deliciously easy recipes for cooking with herbs, includes zingy sauces, salsas and dressings, plus substantial salads, soups, main plates, sweet things and baking. The recipes celebrate herbs in all their beauty and variety – from sorrel and sage to tarragon and thyme – helping you make the most of them in your cooking.

A herb glossary is included to help you get to know each individual herb, outlining the distinctive qualities, from scent to texture and taste. Additionally, information on how to grow your own herbs is also featured, with step-by-step instructions and advice on how to get the best from your herb garden. Of course, using shop-bought herbs in these recipes will also work beautifully, so don't let any lack of green fingers hamper your cooking or stop you from selecting certain herbs to use in the kitchen.

Scattered throughout the wonderful recipes are interesting snippets of folklore and fact relating to this fascinating family of edible plants. Dive in to this enticing collection and elevate your knowledge of herbs and how to use them to create delicious, herb-focussed dishes.

THE HERBS

With an ancient record in folklore and medicinal history, basil is also a highly distinctive culinary herb, especially in Asian, French and Italian cuisines.

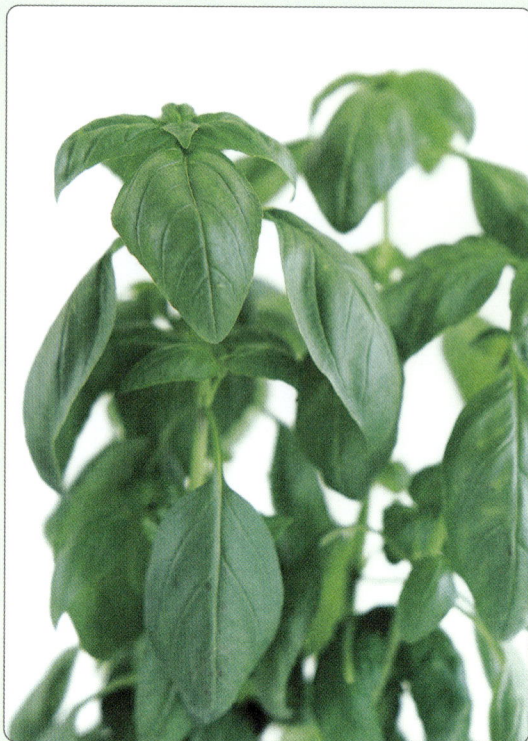

Basil

Ocimum basilicum

Best used freshly picked, basil can also be frozen in leaf form or in made-up sauces. It combines well with tomatoes for a salad and is the main ingredient of pesto sauce for pasta. It adds piquancy to pizzas and to chicken and lamb dishes.

There are at least 13 different types of basil, varying in foliage, colour, shape, texture and aroma. Flavours range from aniseed to cinnamon and the sweet, spicy, clove-like scent of sweet basil. Basil can grow up to 45 cm (18 in).

    O. basilicum 'Purpurascens' has purple leaves and pinkish flowers. *O. basilicum* 'Citriodorum' is lemon scented with green leaves and white flowers. Anise-flavoured basil has pale pink flowers and a strong taste of aniseed. The tiny leaves of Greek basil, which grows in the shape of a small bush, offer the fullest flavour.

    Plant basil in a herb garden or in containers in late summer, when there is no danger of frost or severely cold weather. In the herb garden grow it in a sheltered sunny site in light well-drained soil. If grown in a container, basil should be kept well watered in dry conditions.

    Basil has traditional uses as a digestive aid and herbal tonic, as well as in aromatherapy.

Bay

Laurus nobilis

Glossy dark-green bay leaves are part of the bouquet garni, the traditional herb bundle used to add flavour to savoury dishes. Bay is also a good flavouring for sweet dishes, particularly rice puddings and other milk desserts; its delicate spiciness can be best enjoyed if the milk is simmered gently with the bay leaf before the other ingredients are added.

An evergreen tree with shiny aromatic, spicy leaves, small yellow flowers and black berries, bay can grow to 8 m (26 ft) but is generally slow-growing, and in containers its height is controlled. It can be clipped into geometric shapes or grown as an elegant ornamental standard.

Shaped bay trees in pots are also useful in herb gardens as focal points to mark the meeting of paths or to emphasize a change of height.

Buy young plants and plant them in spring or autumn in rich, well-drained soil. Although bay will tolerate light shade, it prefers full sun. Protect young plants and plants in containers from frost with straw bales, bubble wrap or hessian windbreaks. Cut back any frost-damaged stems in spring. Pick leaves as needed throughout the year.

L. nobilis 'Aurea' has golden leaves and makes an attractive colour contrast in the herb garden. *L. nobilis* 'Angustifolia', the willowleaf bay, is also attractive as a container plant and in the garden.

Infusions made from bay leaves have been used to stimulate appetite or as an aid to digestion.

Bay leaves were the foliage used in wreaths to garland winners and achievers in classical Greece and Rome.

Chamomile

Chamaemelum nobile

This hardy evergreen perennial is distinguished by flowers that resemble daisies, finely cut foliage – and a perfume that takes your breath away. Chamomile is widely used in cosmetics, soothing skin creams and other medications. Its dried flowers can be steeped in hot water to make a relaxing tisane, and it can be used in other sweet recipes. The creeping, non-flowering variety of chamomile tolerates light traffic, making it suitable for covering a short length of path or the ground under a bench.

Grow chamomile in light well-drained soil in full sun. It can reach 20 cm (8 in) in height. Chamomile paths should be kept weed-free or the weeds will overwhelm the chamomile plants, eventually destroying the fragrant pathway.

Non-flowering lawn chamomile, *C. nobile* 'Treneague', which has fern-like leaves, is used to create scented lawns and paths. Upright chamomile, which has daisy-like blooms, is grown in the border for its flowers, which can be used fresh or dried. The double-flowered form, *C. nobile* 'Flore Pleno', is an attractive addition to the garden, and its flowers are used to make chamomile tea.

The flowers of upright chamomile have medicinal and cosmetic uses in facial steam baths and hair rinses; they also bring a soothing and relaxing fragrance to a bath. Dried flowers and leaves of chamomile can be added to potpourri.

A pineapple-like scent floats in the air when the leaves are crushed underfoot or gently squeezed between the fingers.

Chervil is highly prized in France, where it is often used in omelettes/omelets and as a component of the traditional *fines herbes* mixture.

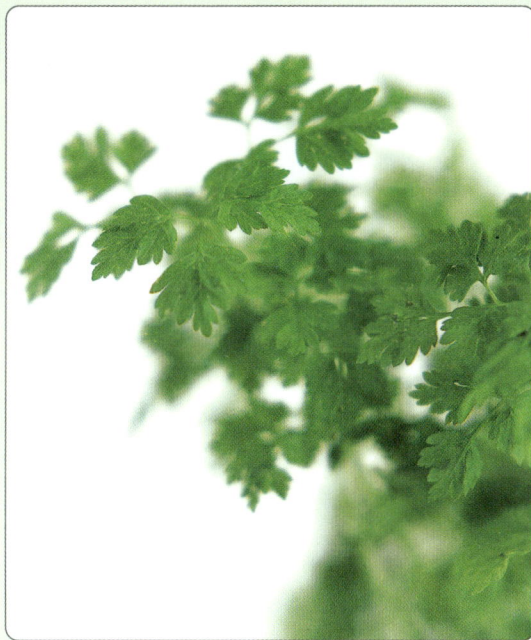

Chervil

Anthriscus cerefolium

A refreshing salad herb, chervil is also useful as a feathery and flavoursome garnish. Its light taste combines well with eggs, poultry and soft cheese. Although best used fresh, the leaves can be preserved by being frozen in ice-cube containers.

Chervil is a hardy annual with pretty fern-like leaves and small white flowers in late summer. It grows up to 60 cm (23 in), thriving in a shady site in light well-drained soil. If planted as an inter-row crop, chervil takes advantage of shade from other row-crop plants. It dislikes root disturbance, so sow it direct into the growing site. Water plants well or they will bolt, flowering and setting seed too quickly, and you will lose flavoursome foliage. Pick the leaves through the summer.

Chervil plants can be grown indoors on a shady north-facing windowsill, but indoor plants will lack the vigour and flavour of plants grown outdoors. You can also sow seed in late summer for a winter crop, which will need some protection through the winter.

Rich in vitamins, chervil has traditionally been used as a treatment for digestive and circulatory disorders.

Chives and Garlic Chives

Allium schoenoprasum and A. tuberosum

Chives have spiky green leaves and mauve flowers, while garlic chives, or Chinese chives, have garlic flavour in their strappy leaves and white starry flowers that appear in late summer. The chopped leaves of both types combine well with egg dishes and are useful for garnishes and in salads. Chives are also among the ingredients of the fines herbes *mixture.*

With their attractive flowers and good foliage, chives fit well into the flower garden. They make an informal edging for part of a kitchen garden and, if planted into spaces in paving, will eventually spread to make their own shapely patterns in the paving gaps.

The spiky leaves shoot from the underground mini-bulbs in spring. They grow to about 30 cm (12 in) but can be harvested once they are about 10 cm (4 in) above ground. Either pull leaves from the clump or cut off a handful with a pair of sharp scissors.

In late spring even spikier shoots carrying the flower buds start to appear. Chive flowers come in a range of pinky-mauve tones, as well as in a new form that is green to white. The flower heads, made up of numerous tiny flowers, are also edible and look attractive in salads. They are at their juicy best just as the buds begin to open.

Chives grow well in containers but will need extra attention to prevent them from drying out. Young plants can be kept on a windowsill or planted out in the sunniest site in the garden.

Coriander/cilantro

Coriandrum sativum

A strongly aromatic, short-lived annual, coriander is grown for its seeds and for its deeply cut, parsley-like leaves that bring spice and flavour to desserts and savoury dishes alike. It bears a profusion of tiny white flowers. For the full effect of their flavour to be appreciated, coriander leaves should be added towards the end of the cooking time.

The pinkish-white flowers that appear from early summer are followed by bead-like seeds, which are used in baking cakes and biscuits as well as in curries, chutneys and pickles. The leaves are added to stews and salads or used as a garnish. Plants grow to a height of about 60 cm (24 in).

In seed catalogues some varieties of coriander may be described as 'slow to bolt', which means they will produce abundant well-flavoured foliage before they flower and set seed. To make sure you have a continuity of leaves, sow a little and often.

Coriander grows well in a sunny spot in light well-drained soil. It needs a long hot summer for best seed production. Sow seeds in spring into the growing site and cover them with a cloche until established. Young plants should be kept well-watered and free of weeds. Pick young leaves before the mature ferny leaves develop.

Seeds tend to fall before they can be harvested, so the flower heads need to be picked before the seeds are fully ripe. Cover the flower heads and store them in a warm, dry, airy place so that the seeds can ripen. Collect and store the seeds in an airtight jar.

Chives (left) bring a hint of onion to garnishes and salads, while coriander/cilantro (right) adds piquancy to curries and other hot dishes.

Dill

Anethum graveolens

An excellent partner for fish in any form, hot or cold, dill is particularly renowned as an ingredient of the Scandinavian marinated-salmon dish gravadlax. Its fresh young leaves bring spice to salads, egg dishes and soups. The seeds, together with the flower heads, are used in pickles, preserves and chutneys. They are tasty with rice and cabbage, or as a flavouring for savoury bread, and are also used ground in curries.

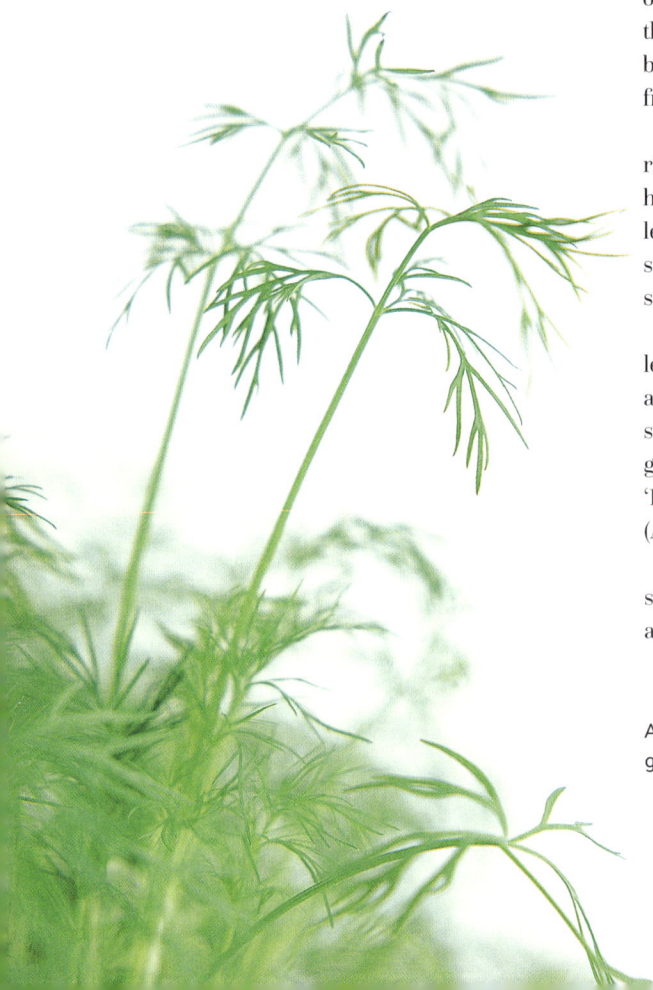

A hardy annual with aromatic feathery leaves and clusters of yellow flowers in midsummer, dill grows to between 60 cm (2 ft) and 150 cm (5 ft), depending on variety. The seed needs well-drained soil, full sun and a sheltered site. Sow in the herb garden in spring, once the soil has warmed up. Since dill grows tall, it is not ideal in containers, but they can be useful for a first sowing.

Water seedlings and thin out to 20 cm (8 in). If necessary, support plants with a light framework of hazel twigs. Water regularly in dry seasons, or the plants will bolt and flower, and leaf harvest will be minimal. Pick leaves as needed when they are fresh and young.

Harvest seeds for culinary use before they ripen completely on the plant. Cut the flower heads off the plant, put them in paper bags and leave them to ripen in a warm dry place. When the seeds are dried, clean off the husks and store the seeds in airtight jars, ready for use.

Many seed companies differentiate between leaf and seed dill. *Anethum graveolens* 'Fernleaf' is a variety grown for high yields of leaves with short stems. *A. graveolens* 'Mammoth' is particularly good for seed production, while *A. graveolens* 'Dukat' is selected for its good leaf production. (All these varieties also produce good seeds.)

Dill is used as a calming treatment for upset stomachs and to alleviate insomnia. Ground seeds are sometimes used as a substitute for salt.

A cleansing spiciness is dill's gift to fish, soups and salads.

Fennel

Foeniculum vulgare

This herb's bright-green leaf shoots unfurl in spring from pale leaf sheaths in which they are tightly packed like small parcels, scented with an unmistakable aroma. Fennel is distinct from Florence fennel, which is grown as a vegetable. The leaves are a flavoursome addition to salads and soups and make a good garnish. Bronze and green fennel can be combined to make a topping for salads. Both types are good partners for fish dishes. The seeds are also used in cooking and to make teas or tisanes. The flower heads can be used in pickling, and the leaves for flavouring oils and vinegars.

Fennel is a hardy perennial grown for its finely cut aromatic leaves in spring and summer and umbels of small yellow flowers in summer. It can grow to more than 2 m (6½ ft) and self-seeds – so be ruthless when you see fennel seedlings in spring. The ornamental quality of its foliage makes bronze fennel, *Foeniculum vulgare* 'Purpurascens', rewarding to grow. It has chocolate-brown feathery leaves, which contrast well with the green of ordinary fennel. The aroma is the same.

Grow fennel in a sunny site in rich well-drained soil. Sow into the growing site in late spring, or in containers in a greenhouse for earlier germination. Either thin or transplant, leaving a space of 50 cm (20 in) between plants.

Pick fennel leaves as needed through the spring and summer. The seeds should be harvested in autumn/fall when they are ripe. Divide established plants of common fennel in spring or autumn. Try to segregate plantings of dill and fennel, or they will cross-pollinate.

Fennel has traditionally been used as a treatment for a wide range of conditions, but it is now most closely associated with the prevention of obesity.

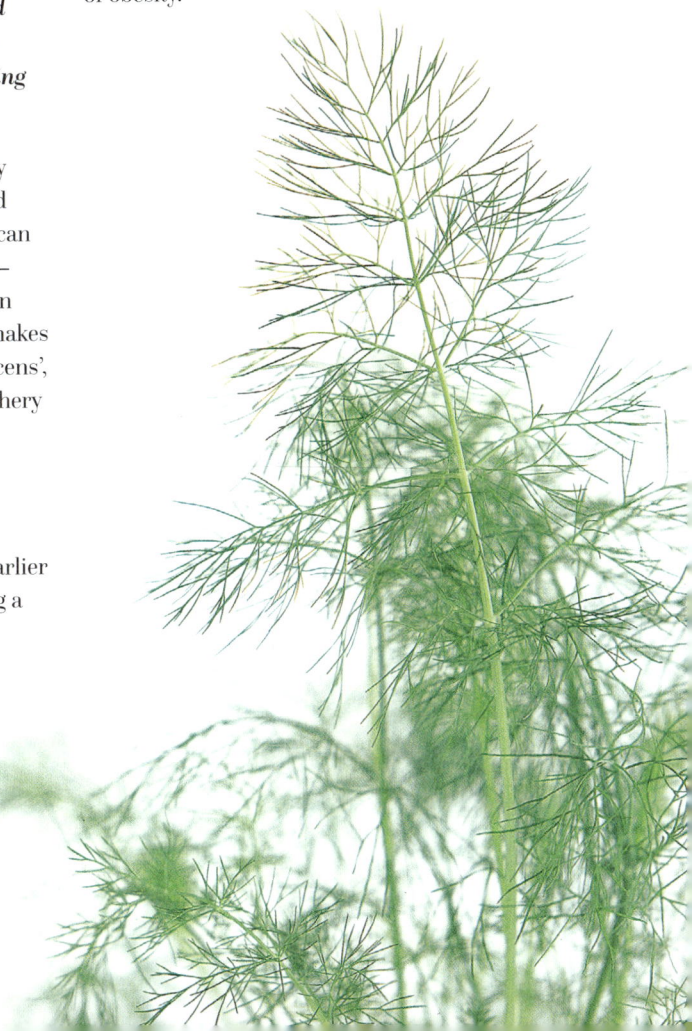

Fennel's wispy foliage is one of the delights of the herb garden in spring.

Individual cloves of garlic can be used whole or chopped, crushed or roasted in their skins to flavour savoury dishes, salads, salad dressings and bread.

Garlic

Allium sativum

Several separate small cloves wrapped in a paper-thin skin that ranges in colour from rose-mauve to white are the components of a garlic bulb. Bulbs bought fresh or home-grown have an unbeatable flavour. Garlic is the main ingredient of many Mediterranean sauces, such as aioli, and is also valued for its health-giving effects.

Garlic has leek- or onion-like foliage and can grow up to 60 cm (24 in). It does best if grown in fertile well-drained soil in a sunny position. Plant individual cloves in spring, in rows 30 cm (12 in) apart, and keep them well watered, especially in dry periods. Lift bulbs in summer and leave them on racks or in wooden boxes to dry off for a day or two in good weather; then hang them up in bunches in a dry, airy shed.

There are several different varieties of garlic available, with varying strengths of flavour; bulb and clove sizes also vary. A. *sativum* has white flowers, while A. *scorodoprasum* (also called rocambole) has a mild-flavoured bulb as well as edible bulbils mixed with flowers on its flower heads. Elephant garlic, A. *ampeloprasum* – which has a huge single onion-like bulb – is often available at supermarkets. Buy several bulbs, some to use and some to plant for next year's crop.

Traditionally used in the treatment of many conditions, garlic has been shown to lower blood pressure slightly and to boost the body's immunity to infections; it also has antiseptic qualities.

Lavender

Lavandula species

Lavender flowers can be used in baking and jam-making or to flavour sugar. More often, the dried flowers and foliage are used to perfume rooms or packed into muslin/cheesecloth sachets and hung up in wardrobes. Flowers destined for potpourri or for making up into lavender bottles or bunches should be harvested as soon as they open, when the colour and aroma are at their most intense.

With grey-green, softly textured, highly aromatic leaves and (depending on species and variety) deep-blue, purple, white or pink flowers, this evergreen shrub grows up to 1 m (40 in). It thrives in a sunny, open site in well-drained, slightly sandy soil. *L. angustifolia* 'Hidcote', which has a uniform, compact shape and produces very deep-blue flowers, is a good choice for edging a path or small border. There are also forms with green, white or red flowers. Some lavenders, including *L. stoechas* and woolly lavender, *L. lanata*, are less hardy and need winter protection.

Lavender is useful as an edging or a hedging plant for a path or small parterre. Provided that you use plants of the same species or variety, the uniformity of shape and colour make it useful in formal as well as informal situations. It tolerates clipping into a variety of shapes. Cut back any woody stems in autumn/fall and remove spent flower heads left on the plant from the previous season's flowering. Sow fresh seed in late summer or autumn. Transplant seedlings to 60 cm (24 in) apart or 30 cm (12 in) if growing as a hedge. Take cuttings in summer.

Lavender has been used therapeutically for its calming effects, as well as in the production of cosmetics and perfumes.

Long valued for its cleansing properties, and associated with fresh-smelling linen, lavender takes its name from the Latin for 'to wash'.

Lemon balm

Melissa officinalis

A powerful lemon scent, released when its leaves are brushed against, and a fresh zesty flavour help to tip the balance in favour of lemon balm, which can become invasive in a small garden. It grows in soft mounded shapes that suit the front of a border. Leaves of lemon balm give a strong citrus flavour to salads.

Lemon balm is a hardy perennial, growing to 1 m (40 in) when in flower. Its rather insignificant flowers are carried on untidy-looking stems from the height of summer to autumn/fall. Lemon balm can be useful for areas in shade, as long as it is planted in well-drained but moist soil.

The *Melissa officinalis* plant has plain green leaves. *M. officinalis* 'Aurea' is a golden-and-green variegated form that is very useful for introducing bold splashes of colour to the herb garden. *M. officinalis* 'All Gold' has yellow foliage.

The variegated form of lemon balm in particular combines well with other plants, but its flower stems should be snipped off to encourage leaf production. Once the flowers have formed, the yellow variegation tends to deteriorate.

Cut back flowering stems in late autumn to contain the tendency to self-seed. Pick leaves when required for fresh use and to dry or freeze. Sow seed in spring and divide established plants in autumn/fall or spring.

A few leaves of fresh lemon balm in boiled water make a tasty tea, which has traditionally been used to relieve the symptoms of stress and tension.

To make the most effective herbal tea, harvest lemon balm before it comes into flower, when the essential oils are at their strongest.

Lovage has a height
and stature that
make it useful as
a tall accent plant
at the centre of a
kitchen herb garden.

Lovage

Levisticum officinale

Lovage has a strong spicy flavour and a long history in traditional English cookery. Its foliage slightly resembles that of celery.

A hardy perennial with large dark-green leaves, lovage can grow up to a height of 2 m (6½ ft). Clusters of small pale-ochre flowers, resembling those of parsley, appear in late summer. It does best in a sunny site in rich well-drained soil. Plants should be watered regularly until established.

Lovage looks attractive near angelica, and if grown at the base of a rose will hide the rose's bare stems. Divide plants in spring or autumn/fall every two or three years. Pick leaves when they are needed and seeds when they are ripe.

Lovage adds spiciness to food. Fresh leaves and stalks can be sprinkled into soups and stews for a meaty flavour, or blanched and eaten as a vegetable. Young leaves are delicious in salads and make an elegant garnish for savoury dishes. Seeds are sometimes added to biscuits before baking. They can be crushed and used as an ingredient of mixed-herb marinades, and are valued as a remedy for digestive complaints.

Mint

Mentha species

Chop mint into vinegar and mix it with sugar and a little warm water to make mint sauce, the natural accompaniment for roast lamb. Mint jelly, made with apples and mint, is also satisfying with lamb dishes. In Middle Eastern countries mint is used in cooked and cold food, as well as in drinks such as mint tea.

The genus *Mentha* includes some 25 species of perennials grown for their leaves, which are usually oval to lance-shaped and toothed at the edges. The ornamental flowers, ranging from deep mauve to light pinky-lavender in colour, attract bees and butterflies.

Mint thrives in full sun in well-drained but moist soil. Set young plants out in spring or autumn/fall, and divide clumps that are growing in the ground in autumn. Mint will grow equally well in light shade and, as long as there is a source of water, provides good ground cover. To restrict its rapid sprawling growth, plant mint in a deep plastic or tin container, and sink the container into the ground.

Gingermint (*Mentha* x *gracilis* 'Variegata') has a spicy flavour and green leaves splashed with yellow. Pineapple mint (*M. suaveolens* 'Variegata') has woolly-textured green leaves, marked irregularly with creamy white, usually at the margins. Spearmint (*M. spicata*) and peppermint (*M.* x *piperita*) – both vigorous, spreading plants with attractive flowers – have the flavour traditionally associated with mint. Probably the most highly scented variety is lemon or eau-de-Cologne mint (*M.* x *piperita* 'Citrata'), which has a bronze tone to its leaves and stems. The perfume of its leaves is overwhelming if it is eaten, so it is better enjoyed as an aromatic foliage plant.

Mint is at its most aromatic before it comes into flower, so cut it back to encourage leaf production. Harvest the leaves through the growing season – they can be used fresh or dried, or frozen for later use. Mint may succumb to mint rust, which shows as rusty markings on the leaves. Remove affected plants and burn them, sterilize the soil, and replant with new healthy plants in another part of the garden.

Every herb garden should have at least one type of mint. Mints also have much to offer in the shape of ornamental leaves and flowers.

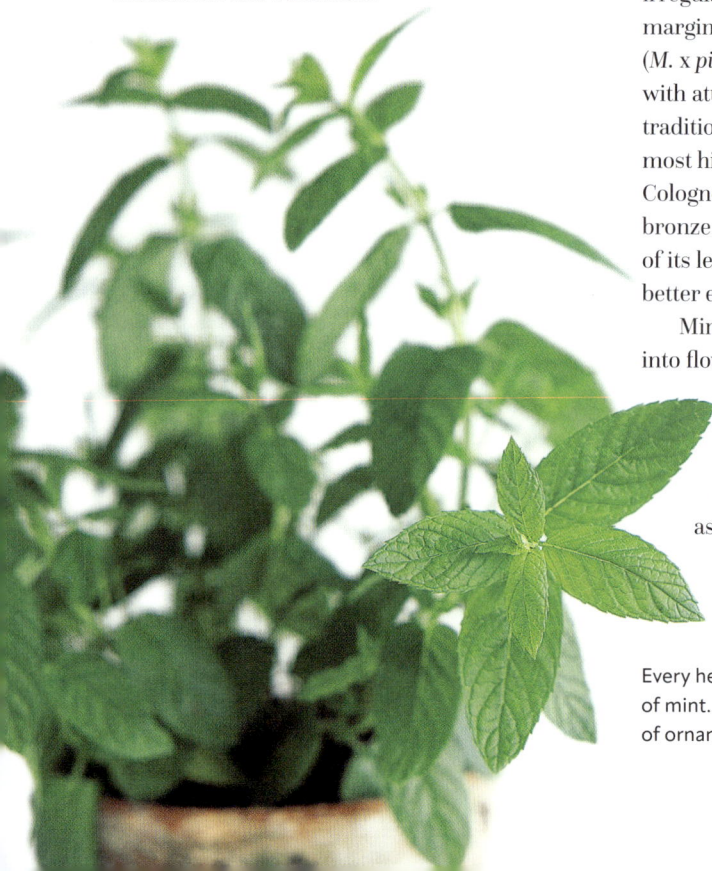

Oregano or Marjoram

Origanum species

Oregano and wild marjoram are two names for Origanum vulgare, *whose spicy aromatic leaves add zest to many meat and tomato dishes, and are an indispensable ingredient in Greek and Italian cuisines. The herb's various types of foliage and flowers also provide subtle ornament in the herb garden.*

There are many other species of marjoram belonging to the *Origanum* genus, the more decorative of which can be used as edging plants or in mixed borders, where their attractive flower stems and aromatic leaves can be readily enjoyed. Some marjorams, including sweet marjoram (*O. majorana*), are half-hardy or tender – either grow them as annuals or protect them in winter.

Golden marjoram (*O. vulgare* 'Aureum') and gold-tipped marjoram (*O. vulgare* 'Gold Tip') provide wonderful splashes of colour in a herb garden. Golden marjoram has clusters of pretty tubular flowers in summer. Its foliage is a lemony-golden colour and makes a good display in the herb garden – but it should be planted in a semi-shady site to avoid leaf scorch from the sun. Gold-tipped marjoram has green leaves tipped with gold, and needs to be grown in a site that is not too shady or it will lose the variegation.

Sweet marjoram (*O. majorana*) forms a compact bushy plant, with a height and spread of about 30 cm (12 in). It needs protection in winter. Its foliage is good used fresh in cooking. Pot marjoram (*O. onites*) has pretty mauve flowers, is a bee magnet and grows to a height of 45 cm (18 in).

Of the several different forms of oregano or marjoram that can be used in cooking, the best is said to be Greek oregano (*O. vulgare* subsp. *hirtum*).

Some plants, including *O.* 'Kent Beauty' and *O. laevigatum* 'Herrenhausen', are generally regarded as decorative plants in the herb garden rather than for culinary use.

Cut back stems after flowering to encourage a flush of new foliage. You can lift and divide to make new plants in spring or autumn/fall.

For cooking, choose Greek oregano, or pot marjoram. The former keeps its flavour when dried, but the latter is better used fresh.

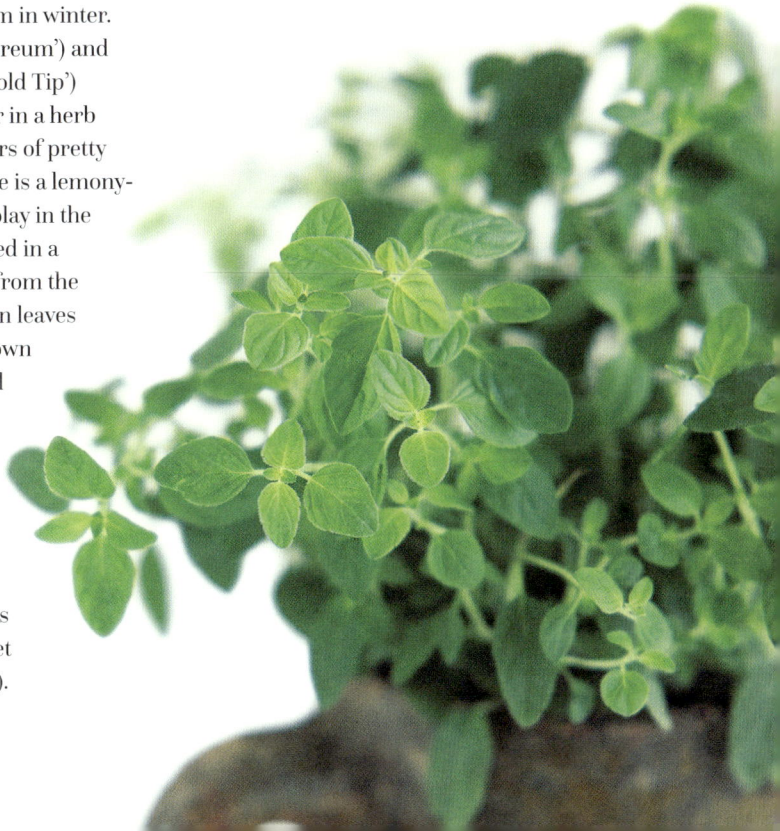

Parsley

Petroselinum crispum

A basic herb of many cuisines, parsley is one of the main components of the bouquet garni herb bundle. You can use the leaves chopped up or whole in salads, as a garnish or as a flavouring for sauces and soups.

There are several varieties of curly-leaved parsley, with tightly curled moss-like leaves. All grow as low compact plants during their first year and flower in their second year. Also attractive, but much larger, is flat-leaved parsley – *Petroselinum crispum* 'Italian', or Italian or French parsley. It grows to a height of 30 cm (12 in). Its foliage is flat, and the stems and leaves are delicious either in salads or in cooked dishes.

Parsley is a hardy biennial that needs to be handled gently when it is transplanted because root disturbance will trigger its survival mechanism and set it in flowering mode too early. It prefers moisture-rich soil and partial shade. Buy plants in spring or autumn. Cover autumn/fall-planted parsley with fleece or a cloche in winter to ensure a good supply of fresh herb.

The chopped leaves of parsley freeze well, and whole leaves can be dried for winter use. You can use parsley to make an alternative to Italian pesto sauce (usually made with basil), for parsley butter and in homemade cosmetics.

It is said that chewing parsley after drinking alcohol or eating garlic freshens the breath.

Part of the traditional bouquet garni, parsley (opposite left) is also a popular garnish, while rosemary (opposite right) is a classic partner for lamb.

Rosemary

Rosmarinus officinalis

The delicate flowers and strongly aromatic leaves of rosemary are ornamental in the herb garden and have long been valued as ingredients in cooking, cosmetics and traditional remedies. The leaves can be dried or frozen for later use.

Rosemary has spiky aromatic leaves on woody branches. It is a hardy evergreen perennial in most areas, but may need protection in harsh winters. Upright forms can reach 2 m (6½ ft) in height, and the prostrate form spreads and trails. Harvest from growing tips to keep the plant bushy and encourage foliage production. Rosemary flowers in summer, with, depending on species and variety, small aromatic blooms in pink, white or blue.

Rosmarinus officinalis 'Prostratus' is a tender trailing or prostrate form with blue flowers. 'Albus' is hardy and has white flowers. For a tall rosemary hedge, choose 'Miss Jessopp's Upright'. 'Silver Spires' is a rediscovered rosemary that was popular in Tudor times; it has silvery variegated leaves and is attractive in any season. 'Majorcan Pink' is half hardy with pink flowers, while *R. lavandulaceus* is tender with blue flowers. 'Sudbury Blue' has delicate blue flowers.

This herb prefers a sunny site with a little protection from cold winter winds. Good drainage is essential. Remove any stems that die back in cold weather and cut back the plant to keep it in shape after flowering. Take cuttings in summer. Pick leaves when needed, but remember that the aromatic flavours are at their best before flowering. Whole stems or sprigs can be dried or frozen for later use. For drying in bulk, harvest in late summer.

Use rosemary flowers and chopped young leaves in salads. Sprigs of rosemary can be laid on joints of meat before roasting; the leaves are added to herb butters, jams, jellies and summer drinks, and are used to flavour sugar for desserts. Rosemary salt is good for seasoning meats and marinades. The herb is an ingredient of some homemade and proprietary skin cleansers and hair conditioners.

Sage

Salvia officinalis

Sage has been grown as a medicinal and culinary plant since ancient times. The name Salvia *comes from the Latin word* salvere, *meaning to heal or save, and common sage – known for its astringent qualities – has been widely used as an antiseptic and cleansing herb in remedies and cosmetic preparations. Gargling with an infusion of sage can help to relieve the pain of a sore throat.*

A hardy evergreen shrub with aromatic and decorative leaves, sage is as versatile in the kitchen as it is ornamental in the flower garden. It is used in numerous meat dishes, sometimes mixed with onion, and in salads, as well as in flavouring salt, oil and vinegar.

There are many sages that look decorative when used in the border, including *Salvia officinalis* 'Tricolor' with leaves variegated in purple, pink and white. Common sage has greyish-green leaves. Purple or red sage ('Purpurascens') has purple-grey leaves, while golden sage ('Icterina') has golden-green leaves.

Sages like full sun, an open site and light well-drained soil. Replace plants that become too woody. Take cuttings in spring or mid-autumn/fall, or layer branches in situ. Common sage and its varieties can be grown from seed, sown direct into the growing site when danger of frost is past, or in seed trays, cells or plugs, where temperatures of 15–21°C (59–70°F) will ensure germination after two or three weeks. If you are growing sage primarily for its leaves, cut out the flowering stems; pick leaves whenever you need them for cooking.

The classic herb for pork dishes, sage is often combined with apple sauce to form one of the best-known partnerships in English cuisine.

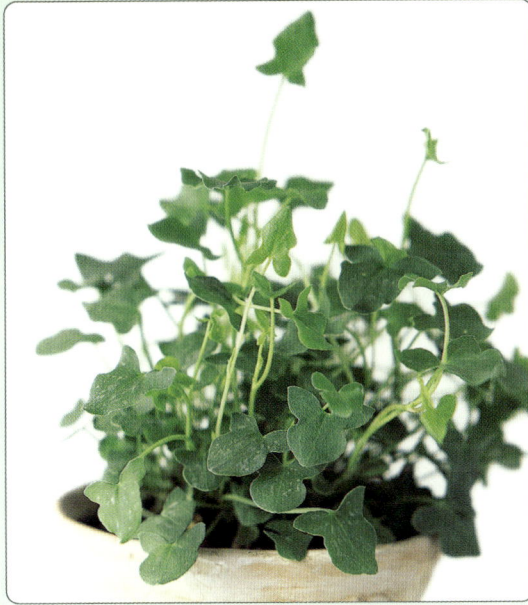

Sorrel is one of the unsung treasures of the herb garden, especially when included in a sauce to serve with oily fish. Its tangy leaves can also be chewed to relieve thirst.

Sorrel

Rumex acetosa

Sharp and clean to the taste, sorrel is an often undervalued element of the herb garden. Made into a sauce, it is a refreshing accompaniment to oily fish and adds piquancy to casseroles and stews. Buckler leaf sorrel (pictured), which has a milder taste, is particularly good in salads or as an alternative to spinach.

One of the traditional herbs of French cuisine, sorrel is a herbaceous perennial that, once established, will be in the herb garden for ever. It dies down in winter, but in spring its fresh green leaves appear – and at that time are at their tangy best for use in salads or sauces.

There are two sorrels that are useful in the kitchen and the garden. Common sorrel or garden sorrel (*R. acetosa*) is a strong-growing herb that makes large clumps of shield-shaped leaves, which should be eaten before the plant flowers; tall stems shoot up from the leaf mounds in summer, and the leaves on these stems do not taste as good. Small, unremarkable blooms are carried at the ends of the branched flower stems.

Of greater attraction in the garden is buckler leaf sorrel or French sorrel (*R. scutatus*). This comes in a green form and a more interesting silver-variegated form, 'Silver Shield', which has a marbled silvery centre to the leaf and gives good ground cover.

Sorrel is valued mainly for its culinary attributes, and has been used to treat blood disorders, but it has a high oxalic acid content and, if consumed in large quantities, may be harmful, especially to the kidneys – so use with caution.

Tarragon

Artemisia dracunculuss

The fiery aniseed flavour of tarragon makes it perfect for spicing meat and fish dishes. The leaves also add piquancy to oils and vinegars and are excellent in marinades. Pick the leaves during spring and summer to use fresh, and in late summer to freeze for winter use.

French tarragon is a hardy perennial with lance-like, narrow, pale greenish-grey leaves. It can grow to a height of 90 cm (3 ft). In warm climates it may produce small flowers. In cold climates it doesn't flower and propagation is from stem cuttings in spring or root cuttings in autumn/fall.

Grow tarragon in light well-drained soil in a sunny site, and cut it back in autumn. Protect the crown with a covering of conifer foliage or straw during winter. Divide plants in spring or autumn.

There is a less tasty but more vigorous form of the herb called Russian tarragon (A. *dracunculoides*), which is often sold wrongly labelled as French tarragon. This species is very hardy and will survive winters without protection, but it is worth growing French tarragon for its flavour, which is far superior to that of the Russian variety.

Although it has no modern medicinal uses, tarragon was once valued as an antidote to snake bites.

Tarragon packs a powerful punch in its narrow lance-like leaves. Often teamed with chicken, it is also the herb used to make sauce Béarnaise.

Thyme

Thymus vulgaris

An evergreen that can be used freshly picked all through the year, thyme is a component of bouquet garni. Both the flowers and the leaves are good in salads and are used to flavour oils, vinegars and marinades, as well as stocks and stews. Thyme is commonly added to stuffing for chickens. It combines particularly well with rosemary.

Thyme is a hardy evergreen sub-shrub with small, powerfully aromatic, spike-shaped or round leaves. There are variegated silver and golden forms.

The most vigorous and most useful for basic flavouring is common thyme (*T. vulgaris*), which has deep-green leaves and is a many-branched woody sub-shrub, with mauve flowers. *T. vulgaris* 'Silver Posie' has silver variegated leaves and a good flavour. *T.* x *citriodorus* is a shrubby thyme, with green lemon-scented leaves and pink flowers.

T. x *citriodorus* 'Silver Queen' is variegated with creamy silvery leaves, rosy-pink buds and a strong lemon scent to its leaves. *T. serpyllum* 'Snowdrift' is a creeping thyme that carpets the ground in white when in flower.

The herb is versatile, which means it can be grown equally well in the garden, on rockeries or in containers. The low-growing forms can be used to make attractive flowering paths or fragrant mats at the feet of benches. On a patio, plant up the cracks or gaps between paving slabs to make aromatic stepping stones.

Both upright and creeping forms of thyme produce aromatic leaves and attractive clusters of small pink, mauve or white flowers, which are as useful as the foliage in flavouring food.

Grow thyme in full sun in well-drained soil. After flowering, cut back the plant to promote new growth and bushy shapes. Replace plants every few years, when they become too woody and open at their centres.

Thyme has traditionally always been used as an antiseptic.

How to Grow Herbs

Herbs are versatile plants that grow well in most types of garden soil and in most conditions. Their numbers can be increased by dividing plants or taking cuttings. Seed can often be sown direct into the ground – or you can sow it in pots and grow the new plants in windowsill propagation units or in a greenhouse.

Sow seed of hardy annuals direct into the soil in spring either in a seedbed or in their growing sites. Half-hardy herbs can also be sown in their growing sites once all danger of frost is past. Sow the seed in rows and just cover it with soil, then water in well and thin out when seedlings are well established.

Sowing indoors produces plants ready for planting out as soon as the soil warms up and the seedlings have been hardened off in spring. Almost fill seed trays or cellular modules with soil, firm the surface down and water the compost or stand the trays in water. Leave the trays to drain before sowing fine seed into the compost surface. Space out large seeds and sieve a thin covering of compost over them. Put the trays in a heated propagator, with an even temperature of 15°C (59°F). Once the seeds have germinated and are large enough to handle, transplant them into small individual pots. Harden off by leaving them outside during the day and returning them to the greenhouse at night, until they are acclimatized to outdoor conditions.

Before buying a herb that is ready to plant out in the garden or to grow indoors, check that it has no obvious disease or pest problems; avoid plants that are root-bound or have damaged stems. Plant out your new herb as soon as possible, but not during the hottest part of the day. Dig a hole large enough to take the root ball, and remove any weeds from the soil. Put the plant in the hole, backfill with soil, then firm the surface of the soil and water the plant well. In dry conditions water the plant daily until it is well established.

Evergreen herbs such as bay, rosemary, sage and thyme can be harvested from outdoor and indoor herb collections all year, as can herbs that

LEFT Use clean scissors to harvest herb flowers such as lavender. Cut low down on the stem, so that you have long stems to tie into bundles for drying. Harvest on dry days, when the sun has just burnt off the dew, before it gets too hot. Lay the harvested material into a trug or basket and keep it in the shade until you are ready to use it. Harvest only the amount that you can work with in a short time, or the flowers may begin to deteriorate and wilt.

SEQUENCE STARTING FROM TOP LEFT Put a label in place before you sow. Empty the seed packet into your hand and then take a pinch of seed, or one seed if they are large, and place it in the trench or hole. Just cover the soil and firm it down with the back of your hand. Mark the line of the row with a trail of coloured gravel, especially if sowing parsley, which is notoriously slow to germinate.

you have forced into growth in winter, such as mint, tarragon and chives. Annual herbs, including basil, dill and coriander/cilantro, are at their best in spring and summer. Since herbaceous perennial herbs including fennel, lovage and comfrey die back in winter, their harvest period is during the spring and summer.

When each plant has produced good leafy growth, harvest it in an even way, to maintain a well-defined shape. For a handful of leaves to add to salads or cooked dishes, pick the herbs just before you want them, at any time of day.

To promote the growth of your herbs or to increase their numbers, divide the plants in early spring when they are still dormant, or in autumn/

fall when the growing season is coming to an end. Before dividing, cut back all the spent flowering stems. Use a fork to lever the clump out of the ground, lift it out and place it on the soil surface.

The traditional way to divide large plants is to place two forks back to back in the centre of the clump and prise the two sections apart. Repeat until you have reduced the size of the original clump and produced several new sections ready for replanting. Herbs such as chives can be prised apart by hand. Most perennials, such as marjoram, chives, echinacea, tarragon, sorrel, creeping thyme and lovage, grow to form large basal clumps. The growth at the centre becomes weak, and leaf production usually declines.

When the clump is divided, any unhealthy-looking sections can be discarded, which allows the new plant or division to grow healthy new shoots from the rootstock around its edge.

By taking cuttings from individual plants you can produce many new plants for your herb garden. You can use a cutting to reproduce exactly the plant from which you have taken the cutting.

To take a softwood cutting, start by looking for strong and healthy new shoots as soon as the herbs begin to grow in spring. Cut them away from the parent plant with a sharp knife and, if you are taking several cuttings, put them in a plastic bag to keep them moist and cool, and to prevent them

SEQUENCE FROM LEFT Unless they are in a very large and congested clump, chives can easily be divided by hand. Dig up and divide the clump into smaller sections by gently pulling it apart. Discard dead or damaged material. Replant smaller sections in prepared planting holes. Backfill and firm in soil at the surface. Trim the tops of the newly divided plants and water them. Keep the row weed-free and in a short time you will have a crop of fresh chives.

from wilting. Prepare several pots or trays with a good, well-drained cuttings compost. Make a clean cut on the stem of each cutting just below a leaf node, so that each is 10 cm (4 in) long. Cut the lower leaves off each cutting, but leave a few leaves on the stem. Make holes in the compost with a dibber, and put the cuttings in the holes up to the level of the remaining leaves.

Label each cutting with name and date, then put the pot of cuttings in a heated propagator or a mini greenhouse made of a plastic bag. Check the cuttings daily; if using a plastic bag, take it off and turn it inside out every day.

When roots start to appear on the underside of the pot – between a fortnight and four weeks – begin to apply a foliar feed. When the plants are large enough, pot them on into individual pots. Pinch out the growing tips of leafy shoots to encourage a bushy habit.

The method for taking hardwood cuttings is similar to that for taking softwood ones, but hardwood cuttings prefer a very well-drained compost and, since they are taken later in the year – in autumn/fall, when the stems are hard and woody – they need to be overwintered in cold frames or greenhouses before they can be planted out the following autumn. The rooting time for hardwood cuttings is much longer than for softwood cuttings.

A simple way to propagate or increase herbs is to take root cuttings in spring or autumn from healthy looking plants. Mint, bergamot, lemon balm, horseradish, comfrey and sweet woodruff are among the herb plants that can be increased in this way.

Unless they are grown in crowded situations where there is no free circulation of air, or the plants are kept either too wet or too dry, herbs usually remain free of pests and diseases. It is preferable to use organic methods rather than proprietary insecticides or fungicides to deter pests from food plants such as herbs. Many organic gardeners use a proprietary organic soap to make a soapy liquid to use on whitefly or greenfly infestations. Brown spots on mint and chive foliage are symptoms of a disease called mint or onion rust. Plants that are badly affected should be dug up and removed from the herb garden, so that other plants are not infected. You can also sterilize the soil around mint plants to prevent this disease from occurring: place a layer of straw around the affected plant and set the straw alight – but take great care to ensure that the fire does not spread.

Seedlings of basil and other herbs are prone to damping off and dying in the early stages of growth. Deterrents include good air circulation, hygienic conditions, judicious watering, and drenching the compost with a fungicidal compound before sowing.

Scale insects may be a problem on the evergreen leaves of bay grown in containers indoors. Use a soapy liquid to wipe the leaves, and dislodge the scale insects with the head of a cotton bud.

Vine weevil, whitefly and red spider mites may be persistent in protected environments, but can be controlled using soapy sprays or biological controls. Eelworms or nematodes are used for vine weevil, a parasitic wasp called *Encarsia formosa* for whitefly, and *Phytoseiulus persimilis* for red spider mites.

Many herbs self-seed abundantly. Others can be increased by dividing clumps, taking cuttings or sowing fresh seed in spring.

SAUCES & DRESSINGS

This dressing is similar to the traditional Japanese dressing served over wilted spinach. The toasted sesame seeds add a nutty, smoky flavour, which works in beautiful contrast to the freshness of the coriander/cilantro. It is delicious tossed through a mixed noodle and vegetable salad with avocado and tomatoes. If preparing ahead, make sure to give it a really good shake before using.

Coriander & toasted sesame dressing

2 tablespoons sesame seeds
2 large spring onions/scallions, trimmed and chopped
1 tablespoon chopped coriander/ cilantro leaves
1 teaspoon caster/superfine sugar
1 tablespoon rice wine vinegar
1 tablespoon light soy sauce
3 tablespoons sunflower oil
2 teaspoons sesame oil
salt and freshly ground black pepper

Makes 150 ml/2/3 cup

Dry fry the sesame seeds in a small frying pan/ skillet over a medium heat until toasted and starting to release their aroma. Cool and transfer to a food processor. Blend to a paste with the spring onions, coriander, sugar, vinegar, soy sauce and a pinch of salt. Add the oils and blend again until amalgamated. Adjust seasoning to taste and serve.

The combination of orange, dill and walnut oil is lovely and makes a wonderful dressing for smoked fish salads. You can vary the oil and use hazelnut or extra virgin olive oil, if preferred.

Dill & orange with walnut oil

grated zest and juice of 1 orange
1 small shallot, finely chopped
1 small garlic clove, peeled and crushed
1 tablespoon red wine vinegar
4 tablespoons walnut oil
1 tablespoon chopped dill
salt and freshly ground black pepper

Makes 150 ml/2/3 cup

Put the orange zest and juice, shallot, garlic, vinegar and salt and pepper in a bowl and whisk together. Gradually whisk in the oil until the dressing is amalgamated. Stir in the dill to finish.

Serve over frisée lettuce leaves with flaked smoked trout, blanched fine green beans and lightly toasted chopped walnuts.

Based on the classic Italian sauce, this dressing is thinned a little with boiling water to give a pouring consistency suitable to dress salads. It is best used straight away while the mint remains a bright green colour, but if you want to make it ahead of time, omit the lemon juice until just before serving.

Mint salsa verde

½ bunch of mint leaves, roughly chopped
1 garlic clove, peeled and crushed
1 tablespoon drained capers
2 stoned/pitted green olives, chopped
2 teaspoons lemon juice
½ teaspoon caster/superfine sugar
5 tablespoons extra virgin olive oil
1 tablespoon boiling water
salt and freshly ground black pepper

Makes 125 ml/½ cup

Put the mint leaves, garlic, capers, olives, lemon juice, sugar, salt and pepper in a food processor and blend until as finely chopped as possible. Add the oil and water and blend again until you have an evenly blended, vibrant green dressing. Adjust seasoning to taste.

This is fabulous poured over a char-grilled lamb salad with haricot beans, steamed potatoes and rocket/arugula leaves.

Chipotle chillies/chiles have a wonderfully smoky flavour and aroma, giving this dressing a beautiful rich quality. You can buy dried chipotle chillies if you prefer but the paste, available from specialist food stores, is perfect for dressings. Both agave syrup and pumpkin seed oil will be available in health-food stores.

Mexican lime, coriander & chipotle chilli dressing

1–2 teaspoons dried chipotle chilli/chile paste
grated zest and juice of 1 lime
1 teaspoon agave syrup
3 tablespoons pumpkin seed oil or avocado oil
1 tablespoon chopped coriander/cilantro
salt and freshly ground black pepper

Makes 75 ml/⅓ cup

Combine the chilli paste, lime zest and juice, agave syrup and a little salt and pepper in a bowl and whisk until smooth. Gradually whisk in the oil until smooth, stir in the coriander and serve.

Try drizzling this dressing over a chicken, corn and avocado salad on a warm tortilla.

The beauty of travelling is discovering the tastes and flavours of other countries' cuisines and Greece will forever be about simple everyday ingredients transformed by the sun – big juicy tomatoes and sweet sliced onions topped with brilliant white feta and a scattering of dried 'rigani'. Greek oregano in full bloom reaches almost half a metre in height and has small white flowers. It is cut and dried in long stalks, often with the flowers still attached, and it is universally considered the king of oregano. You can buy packets of 'rigani' in specialist food stores.

Greek oregano dressing

6 tablespoons Kalamata olive oil
1 tablespoon red wine vinegar
2 teaspoons 'rigani' or dried oregano
salt and freshly ground black pepper

Makes 75 ml/¹/₃ cup

Place all the ingredients in a screw-top jar and shake well until amalgamated. Allow to rest for 30 minutes for the oregano to soften. Shake again and serve.

Serve with a classic Greek salad of tomatoes, onion, green or black olives and feta.

This dressing is similar to a salsa verde or green sauce. It is a vibrant green colour and is great stirred through a pasta, tuna and tomato salad.

Parsley & green olive dressing

3 tablespoons chopped parsley
10 stoned/pitted green olives, roughly chopped
¹/₂ shallot, chopped
1 small garlic clove, crushed
1 tablespoon white wine vinegar
125 ml/¹/₂ cup extra virgin olive oil
1 tablespoon hot water
salt and freshly ground black pepper

Makes 125 ml/¹/₂ cup

Place the parsley, olives, shallot, garlic, vinegar and a little salt and pepper in a blender and purée until fairly well chopped. Add the oil and water and blend again until you have a vibrant green sauce. Adjust the seasoning and serve.

Chive & shallot dressing

1 shallot, very finely chopped
1 tablespoon chopped chives
1 small garlic clove, crushed
6 tablespoons avocado oil
1 tablespoon lemon juice
a good pinch of caster/granulated sugar
salt and freshly ground black pepper

Makes 125 ml/½ cup

Avocado oil has the most gorgeous deep green luminosity to it, making this a really striking looking dressing. The flavour of avocado oil, however, is milder than extra virgin olive oil and works really well with the shallot and fresh chives in this dressing.

Place all the ingredients in a screw-top jar, seal the lid and shake well until the dressing is amalgamated. Adjust the seasoning and serve.

Serve this dressing with a crisp bacon and cos/Romaine lettuce salad with garlic croutons.

Dill & horseradish dressing

2.5-cm/1-in. piece of horseradish root, peeled (or 2 teaspoons grated horseradish)
1 tablespoon sour cream
1 tablespoon lemon juice
1 tablespoon chopped dill
5 tablespoons extra virgin olive oil
salt and freshly ground black pepper

Makes 200 ml/3/4 cup

Use fresh horseradish if you can as the flavour and texture of the root are superior to that found pre-grated in jars – until grated, the root itself has little aroma but as soon as the flesh is damaged the enzymes break down to produce a mustard oil. The grated flesh must be used immediately.

If using horseradish root, finely grate the flesh into a bowl (or simply spoon in the pre-grated) and stir in the sour cream, lemon juice, dill and a little salt and pepper. Then whisk in the oil until the dressing is thickened and smooth. Adjust the seasoning and serve.

This dressing is delicious with a smoked fish and beetroot salad.

A fresh, herby and zingy dressing full of earthy oregano flavours that goes perfectly with any Greek-inspired dishes or salads.

Lemon & oregano dressing

juice of 2 lemons
1 teaspoon dried oregano
1 garlic clove, crushed
pinch of sea salt
1 teaspoon freshly ground black pepper
1 teaspoon Dijon mustard (optional)
squeeze of runny honey (optional or to taste)
200 ml/3/4–1 cup extra virgin olive oil

Makes enough for 1 salad

Whisk together the lemon juice, oregano, garlic, salt and pepper and mustard and honey, if using, in a medium bowl. Continue whisking while adding the oil in slow, steady stream. Cover and refrigerate until ready to use (best used fresh).

Serve with roughly chopped beef tomatoes, chopped cucumber, crumbled feta, sliced red onions and fresh parsley.

This is the perfect vinaigrette for using up any herbs you may have lurking in the fridge. Use the selection suggested below, or experiment with whatever you have to hand to create this versatile dressing.

Herb vinaigrette

2 spring onions/scallions, chopped
1 garlic clove
3 tablespoons apple cider vinegar
2 tablespoons lemon (or lime) juice
large handful of mixed herbs (parsley, basil and a little thyme and mint)
60 ml/1/4 cup olive oil
1/4 teaspoon cayenne pepper
1/2 teaspoon sea salt
1/4 teaspoon black pepper

Makes enough for 1 salad

Put the spring onions, garlic, apple cider vinegar, lemon juice, herbs, olive oil, cayenne, salt and pepper in a food processor and blend until smooth. Store in the fridge until ready to use (best used fresh).

Serve with classic salad leaves, such as cos lettuce, lollo rosso, spinach and sliced radishes.

For that extra drizzle of something vibrant to any dish, be it over burrata, finishing pasta or over a pizza, then this parsley oil adds an extra dimension. The oil can be used in a vinaigrette, in cold soups or to garnish chicken or fish.

Parsley oil

100 g/3¹/₂ oz. flat-leaf parsley
3 garlic cloves, coarsely chopped
125 ml/¹/₂ cup extra virgin olive oil

Makes 1 small jar

Put the parsley and garlic in a food processor or blender and blend until coarsely chopped. With the motor running, gradually add the oil and process until very smooth. Transfer to a muslin/cheesecloth-lined sieve/strainer placed over a bowl and set aside until all parsley oil has drained through. Discard the solids and decant the oil into a sterilized bottle. It will keep in the fridge for 1 week.

Making a batch of this garlicky and herby butter will transform your cooking. It's perfect for keeping in the freezer and using a little (or a lot!) whenever you need a herby hit in your cooking.

Garlic & herb butter

2 garlic cloves
10 g/¹/₃ cup mixed herbs (parsley, coriander/cilantro, mint, tarragon)
100 g/1 stick minus 1 tablespoon unsalted butter, at room temperature

Makes 100g/3¹/₂ oz.

Peel and grate the garlic and finely chop the herbs (removing any hardy stalks).

Add a third of the butter to a small saucepan over a low heat and let the butter melt. Once melted, add the garlic, let it loosen and heat up into the melted butter for a minute.

Remove from the heat and then add to a heatproof bowl with the remaining butter, the herbs and a pinch of seasoning, mixing with a spoon to combine.

Once everything is incorporated, leave to cool, then roll into a log in some parchment paper and transfer to the freezer.

When you want some, just chop off a chunk and re-cover the exposed end with parchment paper. Return to the freezer and use again soon!

Pistachio pesto

200 g/7 oz. shelled unsalted
pistachio nuts
1 garlic clove
50 g/3/4 cup pecorino cheese, grated
50 g/3/4 cup Parmesan cheese, grated
handful of basil
handful of flat-leaf parsley
4 tablespoons olive oil
sea salt and freshly ground black pepper

Serves 4

BASIL

Basil isn't just significant for its taste. It can often be recommended to help soothe headaches, sore throats, coughs and skin irritations due to it's high content of vitamins A, C and K, as well as containing calcium, copper and magnesium.

Sicily is the only place in Italy where pistachios are grown. The Arabs, who once controlled the region, are responsible for bringing pistachio trees to Sicily from the Middle East. The Sicilian word for pistachio is *frastuca*, derived from the Arab *fustuq*, which refers to a forest of pistachio trees. When combined with basil and parsley, pistachios make a delicious pesto that is wonderful on pasta, bruschetta, risotto and much more. It also makes a super gift when packaged in a jar and finished with a pretty bow.

Place all the ingredients in a screw-top jar, seal the lid and shake well until the dressing is amalgamated. Adjust the seasoning and serve.

Serve this dressing with a crisp bacon and cos/Romaine lettuce salad with garlic croutons.

SALADS, SOUPS & LIGHT PLATES

Full of the flavours of summer, this side dish would go well with poached salmon, roast chicken or griddled lamb steaks. If the chive stems are topped with their delicate purple flower heads, use them too, as they add both colour and flavour.

New potato, radish & chive salad with feta dressing

500 g/1 lb 2 oz. baby new potatoes, scrubbed and halved

100 g/3¾ oz. radishes, thinly sliced into rounds

½ cucumber, quartered, seeded and sliced

3 large handfuls of watercress, tough stems removed, torn into small sprigs

handful of chives, including flowers if available

FETA DRESSING

150 g/5 oz. feta, crumbled

125ml/½ cup natural/plain low-fat yogurt

juice of 1 lemon

1 large garlic clove, crushed

2 large handfuls of mint leaves, finely chopped

salt and freshly ground black pepper

Serves 4

Cook the potatoes in plenty of boiling salted water for 12–15 minutes until tender, then drain and transfer to a large serving bowl.

Meanwhile, to make the dressing, blend the feta cheese, yogurt and lemon juice in a blender until smooth and creamy, then pour it into a bowl. Stir in the garlic and mint and season with pepper; you won't need any salt as the feta is salty enough.

Add the radishes, cucumber and watercress to the bowl containing the potatoes. Snip half the chives over and add enough of the dressing to generously coat everything. Toss until thoroughly combined, and serve the salad with the remaining chives (and flowers, if any) arranged over the top.

CHIVES

Chives are a perennial herb, resembling hollow blades of grass. They are the smallest member of the onion family. Make use of the whole plant, flowers and all.

This is delicious served with fish or meat and tastes extra special if the beans and herbs are home grown from your vegetable garden.

Three beans with mint & limes

175 g/1 cup broad/fava beans, shelled
150 g/1 cup runner beans
150 g/1 cup French beans
1 small red onion, finely chopped
zest and juice of 2 limes
2 tablespoons fruity extra virgin
   olive oil
generous handful of mint leaves,
   roughly chopped
salt and freshly ground black pepper

Serves 4

Cook all the beans together in a pan of salted, boiling water, until al-dente – about 4 minutes. Drain and refresh with cold water to prevent any further cooking.

Dress the beans with the onion and lime zest. Mix the oil and lime juice together in a small bowl. Add the salt and pepper. Pour over when ready to serve and scatter over the mint. Adjust the lime juice and oil to suit your taste buds.

Fresh and fragrant, this salad is full of vibrant tastes with its sweet and sour dressing and mass of crisp vegetables and herbs. As a twist, the salad is topped with carpaccio of beef. To make the beef easier to cut into thin slices, freeze it first to firm up and use a very sharp, long-bladed knife. Choose a thick piece of beef, preferably a centre cut.

Vietnamese-style beef salad

200 g/7 oz. sirloin steak
2 handfuls of baby spinach leaves
1 carrot, sliced into thin strips
1 small cucumber, quartered
    lengthways, seeded and cut into
    thin strips
2 handfuls of finely shredded
    red cabbage
2 spring onions/scallions, thinly
    sliced diagonally
handful of Thai basil leaves,
    roughly torn
handful of mint leaves, roughly
    chopped
1 medium red chilli/chile, seeded
    and thinly sliced
30 g/¼ cup roasted unsalted peanuts,
    roughly chopped

VIETNAMESE DRESSING
3 tablespoons groundnut/peanut oil
2 tablespoons fish sauce
juice of 1 lime
1 teaspoon caster/superfine sugar
salt and freshly ground black pepper

Serves 4

Put the steak in the freezer for 30 minutes to firm up and to make it easier to slice.

While the steak is in the freezer, mix together all the ingredients for the dressing and season to taste.

Divide the spinach between 4 serving plates and top with the carrot, cucumber and red cabbage. Spoon enough of the dressing over to coat and toss lightly until combined.

Remove the steak from the freezer and using a very sharp, long-bladed knife, cut into thin, elegant slices. Place the cut slices on a plate and cover with cling film/plastic wrap to prevent them discolouring; if you put cling film between each layer of beef, you will be able to separate them easily.

Arrange the steak on top of the salad, season and sprinkle the spring onions, herbs, chilli and peanuts over the top. Spoon more dressing over to taste, and serve immediately.

This zingy tomato and parsley salad is a Lebanese classic,
traditionally served as a mezze dish and packed full of herbs.

Tomato tabbouleh

1 tablespoon bulgur wheat
350 g/12 oz. ripe but firm tomatoes
100 g/1 cup flat-leaf parsley
1 spring onion/scallion, finely chopped
2 tablespoons thinly sliced mint leaves
juice of 1 lemon
2 tablespoons extra virgin olive oil
salt and freshly ground black pepper
mint sprigs, to garnish

Serves 4

Soak the bulgur wheat in cold water for 15 minutes to soften.

Meanwhile, finely dice the tomatoes, discarding the white stem core. Trim off and discard the stalks of the flat-leaf parsley and finely chop the leaves. If using a food processor, take care not to over-chop the parsley as it may turn to a pulp; you want the parsley to retain its texture.

Drain the soaked bulgur wheat, squeezing it dry of excess moisture. Toss together the diced tomatoes, chopped parsley, bulgur wheat, spring onion and mint. Add the lemon juice and olive oil, season with salt and pepper, and toss well.

Garnish the tabbouleh with mint sprigs and serve at once.

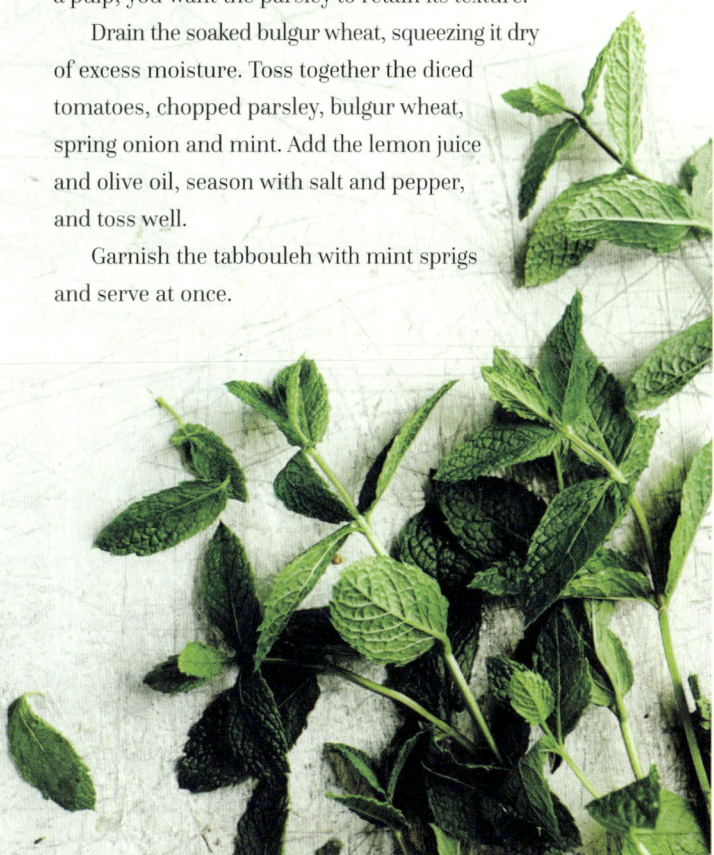

Roasted shallots with a touch of cinnamon serve as a bed for the freekah, mixed fresh herbs, crisp cucumber, tomatoes, olives and intense citrus but yet mellow preserved lemon. For an extra element, crumble over some feta or add pan-fried halloumi.

8 shallots, peeled and halved
2 tablespoons olive oil
pinch of ground cinnamon
pinch of dried oregano
200 g/7 oz. freekah, rinsed
50 g/generous 1/3 cup almonds,
    coarsely chopped and toasted
1 large cucumber, cubed
200 g/7 oz. cherry tomatoes, quartered
1 small bunch each dill, coriander/
    cilantro, mint and parsley,
    leaves picked
salt and freshly ground black pepper
feta or pan-fried halloumi, to serve
    (optional)

DRESSING
100 g/1 cup black olives, stoned/pitted
    and halved
1 preserved lemon, pith and flesh
    discarded, skin rinsed and finely
    chopped
1 garlic clove, crushed
60 ml/1/4 cup olive oil
a pinch of ground cinnamon (optional)
juice of 1–2 lemons, to taste
1 teaspoon honey, or to taste

Serves 4

Freekah & herb salad

Preheat the oven to 180°C (350°F) Gas 4.

Spread the shallots on a small baking sheet. Drizzle with the olive oil, sprinkle with cinnamon and oregano and season to taste. Roast in the preheated oven for 40–45 minutes until tender and caramelized.

Meanwhile, bring 400 ml/1¾ cups water and 1 teaspoon salt to the boil in a saucepan over a medium-high heat. Add the freekah, stir, bring back to the boil and cover with a lid. Reduce the heat to low and cook for 25–30 minutes until the freekah is tender and the water evaporates. Drain and transfer to a bowl.

Mix the dressing ingredients in a serving dish, then add the shallots, freekah, cucumber and tomatoes and mix well. Check for seasoning, then add the herbs and scatter over the almonds. Serve with the addition of crumbled feta or pan-fried halloumi, if you wish.

This soup is perfect for a summer supper party and is so refreshing served chilled. It can also be served warm, topped with grated cheese for a warming yet refreshing soup. It has a vibrant green colour and is lovely swirled with cream to finish. To make the soup as smooth as possible, pass the soup through a moulin or a fine-mesh sieve/strainer.

Chilled broad bean, pea & mint soup

15 g/1 tablespoon butter
1 tablespoon olive oil
1 onion, finely chopped
1 garlic clove, finely chopped
40 ml/2½ tablespoons brandy
200 g/1½ cups frozen peas
200 g/1½ cups frozen broad/
    fava beans
1 litre/4 cups vegetable or chicken stock
4 large sprigs of mint
100 ml/⅓ cup plus 1 tablespoon
    double/heavy cream, plus extra
    to serve (optional)
salt and freshly ground black pepper

Serves 4

Heat the butter and olive oil in a saucepan over a medium heat and sauté the onion until soft and translucent. Add the garlic and fry until lightly golden brown.

Add the brandy and heat for a few minutes to cook off the alcohol. Add the peas, broad beans and stock together with the mint and bring to the boil. Reduce the heat and simmer for about 10 minutes until the peas and beans are soft.

Blend the soup in a blender or food processor, or using a stick blender, until smooth and then pass through the moulin or a fine-mesh sieve/strainer to remove the pea and bean skins. If using a sieve, use a spatula to push it through.

Season with salt and pepper. If you want to make the soup richer, stir in the double cream. Chill in the fridge until you are ready to serve.

To serve, pour the cold soup into four bowls and finish with a swirl of cream and some freshly ground black pepper. For an extra chilled soup, add an ice cube when you serve.

This soup has a light and refreshing taste and is slightly sour with the lemon and yogurt. Make sure that the temperature is low when you add the yogurt, as it can split if the soup is too hot.

Courgette lemon yogurt soup

1 onion, finely chopped
2 tablespoons olive oil
1 garlic clove, finely chopped
300 g/10½ oz. courgettes/zucchini, green or yellow, coarsely grated
1 litre/4 cups chicken or vegetable stock
1 egg
250 ml/1 cup natural/plain yogurt
juice of 2 lemons
1 tablespoon chopped tarragon, plus extra to serve
salt and freshly ground black pepper
croûtons, to serve

Serves 4

In a large saucepan, heat the oil over a medium heat and fry the onion until soft and translucent. Add the garlic and fry until lightly golden brown. Add half of the grated courgette and the stock and simmer for 10–15 minutes until the courgette is soft.

In a bowl, beat the egg with the yogurt. Add a ladleful of the hot stock from the soup and whisk together to warm the yogurt before adding to the soup (this will prevent it from splitting). Add the lemon juice and tarragon to the egg and yogurt mixture, and then whisk it all into the soup. Blend the soup in a blender or food processor until smooth, or use a stick blender.

Return the soup to the pan and add the remaining courgette. Simmer for a few minutes, then pour the soup into four bowls and serve topped with extra chopped tarragon, a sprinkling of black pepper and some croûtons.

TARRAGON

This is a perennial plant, meaning once planted it will grow back every year. The French variety is the most used in cooking, with its glossy, thin leaves and aromatic flavour. Tarragon is a herb that you either love or hate, depending on whether you like the taste of liquorice or not.

This recipe is a close cousin of a Ukrainian dish, and will soon become a regular in your repertoire for its ease, delicious taste and wow factor.

Pickled lox

300 ml/1¼ cups distilled white vinegar
125 g/⅔ cup light brown sugar
25 g/2 tablespoons sea salt
6 bay leaves
2 teaspoons coriander seeds
2 teaspoons yellow mustard seeds
1 teaspoon black peppercorns
1 teaspoon allspice berries
handful of dill, chopped, plus extra
   to garnish
500 g/1 lb. salmon fillet, skin on
1 white onion, finely chopped, optional

TO SERVE
rye bread
cream cheese
chopped dill, to garnish

Serves 8

Put all the ingredients except the salmon and onion into a non-reactive saucepan with 1 litre/1 quart water and bring to the boil. Turn down the heat and simmer for 5 minutes. Leave to cool to room temperature.

Put the salmon in a non-reactive container and pour over the brine. Cover lightly. Put into the fridge and leave for 3 days.

Take out the salmon and cut into thin slices (like smoked salmon), removing and discarding the skin. Put the slices in a shallow bowl with the chopped onion, if using, and about 100 ml/½ cup of the brine. Serve with rye bread and cream cheese, garnished with dill.

The French baking powder used in this recipe is an ingredient widely used in Vietnamese cuisine, especially in fishcakes. It acts as a raising agent and holds the fish together without having to use another ingredient like potatoes, so what you are eating is just fish. These can be wrapped in Chinese mustard greens and dipped in chilli sauce.

Fishcakes with dill

300 g/10½ oz. skinless haddock
   or monkfish fillets, chopped
1 Asian shallot, chopped
1 Bird's Eye chilli/chile
1½ teaspoons sugar
1 teaspoon French baking powder
   (Alsa Levure Chimique 'Alsacienne')
a pinch of black pepper
2 tablespoons cooking oil, plus extra
   for oiling and frying
2 tablespoons fish sauce
1 tablespoon tapioca starch
handful of fresh dill

steamer (optional)

Serves 4

Put all the ingredients in a food processor and process until fine and well combined. Transfer the mixture to a bowl, cover and allow to rest for 1–2 hours or overnight – in which case, put it in the refrigerator.

Rub a little oil onto your hands. Pull small pieces off the rested mixture and roll into balls. Alternatively, shape the mixture into 1 large or 2 smaller patties.

Steam the balls or fishcakes for 5 minutes in a steamer. They can then be refrigerated or frozen, to be fried at a later date. You can also poach them in broth for noodle soups.

To serve, heat a dash of oil in a frying pan/skillet and fry the balls or fishcakes, stirring or turning a couple of times, until golden brown all over. Leave the balls whole, but slice the fishcakes.

Note: Any white fish, salmon or trout can be used in place of the haddock or monkfish.

The richly herb focussed, garlicky dressing works perfectly here with poached eggs, wilted spinach and creamy avocado, cutting through all the flavours, to create a satisfying light plate.

Green eggs, spinach & avocado
with basil & coriander dressing

1 ripe hass avocado
80 g/½ cup cherry tomatoes
200 g/4 cups baby spinach leaves
4 eggs
½ teaspoon white wine or malt vinegar

BASIL & CORIANDER DRESSING
25 g/½ cup basil leaves
10 g/¼ cup coriander/cilantro leaves
60 ml/¼ cup extra virgin olive oil
1 garlic clove
pinch each of salt and freshly ground
   black pepper

a high-speed blender

Serves 2

First, half-fill a large saucepan with water and bring to the boil over a medium heat.

Next, prepare the dressing. Simply add all the ingredients to a blender and whizz until smooth. Leave to one side.

Peel the avocado, remove the stone/pit and chop the flesh into small chunks. Cut the cherry tomatoes in half. Set aside.

Add the spinach to the hot water, leave it to wilt for about 30 seconds, then transfer to a bowl using a slotted spoon – you want to keep the water on the heat as you will use it to cook the eggs in (plus it saves washing up). Once the spinach has cooled a bit, squeeze out the excess water and set aside.

Next, poach the eggs. Set a large saucepan over a medium–high heat. Fill with water to about 7.5-cm/3-inches deep. Add the vinegar, then crack the eggs, one by one, into the water. Get each egg as close to the simmering water as you can before gently cracking the shell to release the egg into the water slowly so it has a better chance of holding its shape. Cook for about 2 minutes, depending on how runny you like the yolks. You can lift the eggs from the water using a slotted spoon and gently touch the yolk to see if it is to your liking.

Arrange the wilted spinach, avocado chunks and cherry tomatoes on serving plates. Using a slotted spoon, carefully remove the eggs, draining off as much water as possible. Lay the eggs on top of the vegetables, drizzle with the dressing, sprinkle with salt and pepper, and serve.

This is simple to make and such a satisfying dish to eat on colder days. The sweet butternut squash contrasts nicely with the dark and earthy lentils, both in flavour and appearance. If you've got some feta lurking in the fridge, throw a few crumbs on top to serve.

Roast squash & lentil salad

1 x 1-kg/2-lb. 4 oz. winter squash, such as butternut, pumpkin, hubbard or acorn
4 tablespoons olive oil
a couple of pinches of dried oregano
a few sprigs of rosemary
6 garlic cloves, unpeeled and halved
1 x 250-g/9-oz. packet of ready-to-eat cooked Puy lentils
1 x 250-g/9-oz. packet of ready-to-eat cooked green lentils
1/2 red onion, thinly sliced
100 g/3½ oz. cooked beetroot/beet, cut into wedges
small handful of chopped flat-leaf parsley
2 tablespoons red wine vinegar, to taste
salt and freshly ground black pepper

Serves 8 to share

Preheat the oven to 200°C (400°F) Gas 6.

Peel and deseed the squash and cut the flesh into 2.5-cm/1-inch slices (if you are using butternut, you can leave the skin on as it will cook okay). Put the squash pieces in a bowl and add a glug of olive oil, the oregano, rosemary and garlic.

Tip into a roasting pan and roast in the preheated oven for about 30 minutes, or until the squash is tender and cooked and starting to brown at the edges.

Tip both the Puy and green lentils into a large bowl and add the red onion, beetroot wedges and chopped parsley. Dress the salad with a generous amount of the remaining olive oil and a splash of red wine vinegar – taste and adjust the balance of olive oil and vinegar to taste. Season with salt and pepper.

Add the roasted squash to the bowl and fold it into the lentils, along with any cooking juices in the pan. Serve straight onto your board or in a serving bowl.

The tarragon used in this delicious pâté perfectly pairs with sardine to cut through the rich taste. Pair with the best seeded crackers you have for a fresh and tasty snack.

Lemon, tarragon & sardine pâté

2 tablespoons olive oil
1/2 red onion, sliced
1 1/2 tablespoons chopped fresh
   tarragon leaves
2 x 120-g/3 3/4-oz. cans of sardines
   in water, drained
pinch each of salt and freshly ground
   black pepper
zest and juice of 1 lemon
2 tablespoons ghee, melted

TO SERVE
toast or seeded crackers
1 cucumber, sliced
lemon wedges
fresh tarragon leaves

Serves 4

Heat the olive oil in a frying pan/skillet over a low–medium heat. Add the red onion and cook for 6–7 minutes until the onion softens and begins to caramelize. Add the tarragon near the end and cook for another minute. Leave to cool slightly, then transfer to a food processor.

Add the sardines, salt and pepper, lemon zest and juice and melted ghee. (There is no need to pick the tiny bones out of the sardines as they will be blended and provide extra calcium.) Blend until you have a smooth pâté.

This is delicious spread on toast or crackers with a few slices of cucumber on top, served with tarragon leaves sprinkled over and lemon wedges to squeeze.

Store in an airtight container in the fridge for 3–4 days.

These falafels are made with chickpeas/garbanzo beans, rye flakes and millet and are high in fibre and protein. Serve them alongside the coriander/cilantro-feta pesto for the perfect snack.

250 g/1½ cups dried chickpeas, soaked overnight in cold water
40 g/scant ½ cup rye flakes, plus 3 tablespoons to finish
60 g/scant ⅓ cup millet, cooked and cooled
2 shallots, chopped
1 green chilli/chile, finely chopped
1 garlic clove, crushed
1 teaspoon each ground coriander, cumin and smoked paprika
½ teaspoon ground cinnamon
½ teaspoon dried chilli/hot red pepper flakes
30 g/1 oz. coarsely chopped mixed flat-leaf parsley and coriander/cilantro
2 tablespoons rye flour
1 teaspoon bicarbonate of soda/baking soda
salt and freshly ground black pepper
vegetable oil, for deep-frying
lime wedges, to serve
1 jar of roasted red (bell) peppers, chopped, to serve (optional)

CORIANDER-FETA PESTO
60 g/3½ cups coriander/cilantro, chopped
50 g/⅓ cup walnuts, chopped
100 g/3½ oz. feta, crumbled
80 ml/⅓ cup olive oil

Serves 4–6

Grainy falafel
with coriander-feta pesto

Drain the chickpeas, discarding the soaking liquid, and process in a food processor with the rye flakes, millet, shallots, green chilli, garlic, spices and herbs until a fine paste forms. Stir through the flour and bicarbonate of soda, and season to taste. Roll the mixture into about 12 walnut-sized balls. Place on a baking sheet lined with parchment paper and refrigerate until chilled.

Meanwhile, to make the pesto, in a food processor blitz the coriander, walnuts and feta into a chunky mixture, then add the olive oil. Mix in the oil, keeping the texture of the pesto chunky.

Fill a medium saucepan with vegetable oil to a depth of 7.5 cm/3 inches. Heat the oil over a medium-high heat until it bubbles softly. Using a slotted spoon, carefully lower the falafel patties into the oil and let them fry for about 3–5 minutes or so until crispy and medium brown on the outside. Avoid overcrowding the falafel in the saucepan and fry them in batches if necessary. Drain on paper towels.

Serve the falafel warm or at room temperature, plated with some coriander-feta pesto, roasted red pepper, if using, and wedges of lime for squeezing.

The beauty of squid is that it takes next to no time to cook – a minute or so is enough, any longer and it becomes tough and rubbery. The zingy herb dressing is the perfect complement to this fresh dish.

Char-grilled squid with herb dressing

60 g/2 oz. mizuna or rocket/
   arugula leaves
100 g/3¾ oz. baby spinach leaves
4 vine-ripened tomatoes, quartered,
   seeded and diced
500 g/1 lb 2 oz. prepared and cleaned
   small squid
2 lemons, halved
2 tablespoons freshly snipped chives
1 red chilli/chile, seeded and cut
   into thin strips

HERB DRESSING

5 tablespoons extra virgin olive oil,
   plus extra for cooking
1 large garlic clove, crushed
2 handfuls of basil leaves
handful of oregano leaves
juice of ½ lemon
salt and freshly ground black pepper

Serves 4

To make the dressing, put all the ingredients in a mini-processor or blender and blend until the herbs are finely chopped. (You could also chop the herbs by hand.) Season the dressing and set aside.

Place the salad leaves on a large serving plate and arrange the tomatoes over the top.

Slice off the squid tentacles, if there are any. Open out the body of each squid and cut in half, then score the skin using the tip of a sharp knife into a diamond pattern. Into a large bowl, pour enough oil to coat the squid lightly and season. Add the squid (including the tentacles) and turn until coated in the oil.

Heat a large, ridged griddle pan over a medium-high heat and sear the lemon halves, cut-side down, pressing them down until caramelized in places. Remove from the griddle and set aside. Next, griddle the squid bodies in batches for 1½ minutes, turning once and pressing them down with a spatula, until cooked and charred in places. Griddle any tentacles, too, for 1 minute, turning once.

Arrange the squid on top of the salad, spoon the herb dressing over the top and garnish with the chives and chilli. Serve the chargrilled lemons on the side for squeezing over.

MAIN DISHES

This delicious treatment of tuna can also be used with sea bass and swordfish. It is always a good idea to get to know your fishmonger as he or she will be able to slice the fresh fish very thinly for you – an opportunity to show off!

Tuna carpaccio with lemon parsley sauce

400 g/14 oz. fresh tuna, cut into
   very thin slices
4 tablespoons extra virgin olive oil
   (not too fruity)
juice of 2 lemons
1 tablespoon chopped oregano
2 tablespoons chopped flat-leaf parsley
250 g/9 oz. rocket/arugula, spinach
   or chicory/endive (or a mixture
   of all three)
salt and freshly ground black pepper
1 unwaxed lemon, sliced, to garnish

Serves 4

Place the tuna on a plate. Whisk together the oil, lemon juice, oregano, parsley and some salt and pepper until emulsified.

Pour the sauce over the tuna. Cover and refrigerate for 1–2 hours, turning once during that period.

Arrange the leaves on a platter, top with tuna and serve garnished with lemon slices.

Baking red mullet in a sealed parchment parcel packed with herbs is an excellent way of retaining the delicate flavour and enticing aroma as it cooks. The flavour is further enhanced by topping the fish with a piquant anchovy butter before baking. Ask your fishmonger to scale and gut the fish, leaving the liver in if possible as this adds to the flavour. If you can't find red mullet, grey mullet will do, or other such fish with fine white flesh.

Red mullet in an envelope

4 red mullet, 200 g/7 oz. each
  (ask your fishmonger to scale,
  clean and gut them for you)
4 herb fennel sprigs
large handful of basil
1 tablespoon rosemary leaves
2 tablespoons olive oil
salt and freshly ground black pepper

ANCHOVY BUTTER
200 g/1¾ sticks unsalted butter,
  softened
8 anchovy fillets in oil, drained

Serves 4

Preheat the oven to 200°C (400°F) Gas 6.

For the anchovy butter, put the softened butter into a bowl, add the anchovy fillets and mash together with a fork. Divide it into 4 pieces and chill until ready to use.

Rinse and dry the fish well and put some of the herbs into the cavity. Cut 4 rectangles of parchment paper large enough to envelop the fish. Brush the fish with olive oil and then place in the centre of a parchment rectangle. Add a piece of anchovy butter to each fish.

Top the fish with more herbs and season with salt and pepper. Bring the long edges of the paper up over the fish and fold together firmly. Twist the ends of the paper to seal. Place the packages on a baking sheet and bake in the preheated oven for 20 minutes.

Serve the fish in their fragrant packages.

This is an adaptable dish, which works for any fish fillets. Because fillets vary in thickness, a good guide is to allow 4 minutes of baking time per 1 cm/½ inch of thickness. You can also vary the topping, according to what herbs, snacks or savoury crackers you have lying around – just be sure to make sure they are well crushed in the first step.

Fish fillets with a dill crust

2 fish fillets, such as salmon, cod
    or haddock, with or without skin
    (about 120 g/4¼ oz. each)
splash of olive oil
2 lemon wedges

TOPPING
15 g/½ oz. cheese biscuits/crackers,
    crisps, pretzels, or other snacks,
    broken into small pieces
    (1 small handful)
3 tablespoons panko crumbs
15 g/1 tablespoon butter
small handful of dill, finely chopped
1 teaspoon creamed horseradish
2 teaspoons mayonnaise

Serves 2

Pulse the cheese biscuits in a small food processor to rough crumbs, add the panko crumbs and pulse again. Melt the butter in a small pan and fry the crumb mixture for 3–4 minutes, until fragrant, golden and lightly toasted. Take off the heat and stir in the dill.

Dry the fish, brush all over with oil and season generously with salt and pepper. Place the fish – if it has skin, skin-side down – in a small rimmed baking pan, lined with foil. Mix the horseradish and mayonnaise and spread evenly on top of the fish, then sprinkle over the crumbs and press on gently. Refrigerate at this point for up to an hour.

Add the lemon wedges to the baking pan and bake at 180°C (350°F) Gas 4 for 13–18 minutes (depending on thickness), checking the centre is translucent when poked with a knife. If you have a digital thermometer, it should read 52°C/126°F. To serve, slide a spatula under each fillet (if the skin sticks to the foil, so much the better), and serve with a hot lemon wedge.

Note: If you have surplus dill, one option is to freeze it. Wash and dry the dill thoroughly and freeze it in a small plastic box, to keep the fronds intact. Chop finely, still frozen, and separate any clumps.

Ideal for relaxed entertaining, you can either cook these on a hot barbecue or under the grill/broiler. Bay leaves, fish and lemon are a flavour-match made in heaven.

Monkfish & bay leaf skewers
with lemon & vegetable slaw

1 kg/2¼ lb. monkfish tails, skinned
24 large fresh bay leaves
olive oil, for brushing
lemon wedges, to serve
salt and freshly ground black pepper

VEGETABLE SLAW
2 red apples
2 carrots, peeled
300 g/2 cups celeriac, peeled and grated
200 g/2 cups Savoy cabbage, finely shredded
handful of flat-leaf parsley, finely chopped
handful of chives, finely chopped
40 g/⅓ cup pecans, roasted and roughly chopped
5 tablespoons buttermilk
5 tablespoons extra virgin olive oil
zest from 1 unwaxed lemon, plus juice from ½

8 bamboo barbecue skewers, soaked in cold water

Serves 4

To make the vegetable slaw, cut the apples and the carrots into small, slim matchsticks. Place the sliced vegetables in a large bowl with the grated celeriac, shredded cabbage, fresh herbs and chopped pecans.

In a separate bowl combine the buttermilk, olive oil, lemon zest and juice. Season to taste with salt and pepper and stir together. Pour onto the vegetables and toss to mix. Set the slaw aside in the refrigerator until ready to serve.

Cut the monkfish tails into 16 even-sized pieces of around 5 cm/2 inches each. Thread three bay leaves and two pieces of monkfish alternately onto each of the pre-soaked bamboo skewers, starting and ending with a bay leaf. Brush the fish with olive oil and season with salt and pepper.

Preheat a barbecue or grill/broiler to medium. Cook the skewers on/under the heat for 2 minutes on each side until the fish is cooked through. Serve with the slaw and lemon wedges to squeeze over.

This cod fillet is pan-fried until the skin crisps up, and then a light lemon butter is sizzled in the same pan, ready to spoon over to serve. White polenta is given an umami-flavour boost with Parmesan, and the whole dish is finished off with the fresh zing of a green herb and garlic gremolata.

Pan-fried cod fillet
with white polenta & basil gremolata

2 teaspoons olive oil
4 x 200-g/8-oz. cod fillets, skin on
40 g/3 tablespoons butter
juice of 1 lemon
large handful of basil, leaves picked
salt and freshly ground black pepper
samphire, to serve (optional)

WHITE POLENTA
1½ litres/6 cups vegetable stock
250 ml/1 cup milk
350 g/2 cups white polenta/cornmeal
3 tablespoons finely grated Parmesan
50 g/3½ tablespoons butter,
   coarsely chopped

BASIL GREMOLATA
finely grated zest and juice of 1 lemon
3 tablespoons olive oil
2 garlic cloves, crushed
½ a bunch of flat-leaf parsley,
   finely chopped
½ a bunch of basil, finely chopped

Serves 4

For the polenta, bring the vegetable stock and milk to a simmer in a saucepan over a medium heat. Add the polenta in a thin steady stream, whisk continuously until all is incorporated, then stir occasionally for about 15–20 minutes until the polenta is cooked through. Stir through the Parmesan and butter. Keep warm while you cook the cod.

For the gremolata, mix together the lemon zest and juice, olive oil, garlic, parsley and basil in a bowl and set aside.

Lightly coat the base of a non-stick frying pan/skillet with olive oil, then place the pan over a medium-high heat. Once the pan is hot, season the cod pieces with salt, then place them in the pan, skin-side down. Cook for 2–3 minutes until the skin is nicely golden and crisp. Carefully turn the cod over and cook for a further 2–3 minutes, depending on the thickness of the fillet or loin. The fish is cooked when the flesh becomes opaque. Add the butter, squeeze over the lemon juice, season with salt and let it bubble and brown.

Serve the cooked cod on warmed plates with the polenta, topped with the gremolata and basil leaves and spoonfuls of the lemon butter and samphire on the side, if liked.

This Sicilian salmoriglio sauce is wonderful with lamb, seafood and swordfish (and even steak). It is easy to make and have ready in the fridge. Oregano is the star of this dish adding a wonderful depth of flavour and earthiness.

Chicken with salmoriglio

1 chicken (preferably organic),
   1.8 kg/4 lb., butterflied
1 tablespoon olive oil
1 tablespoon chopped rosemary
2 garlic cloves, finely chopped

SALMORIGLIO
1 garlic clove, crushed
2 bunches of oregano
   (or 1 good handful)
60 ml/4 tablespoons extra virgin
   olive oil
juice of 1 lemon
salt and freshly ground black pepper
2 lemons, cut into wedges, to serve

Serves 4–6

Place the chicken in a sealable plastic bag with the oil, rosemary and garlic. Season well, seal the bag and massage the chicken through the bag to coat well. Marinate in the fridge for at least 2 hours.

Bring the chicken back to room temperature before cooking. Transfer the chicken to a casserole dish.

Preheat the oven to 180°C (350°F) Gas 4.

Roast the chicken in the preheated oven for 35–40 minutes until browned and the juices run clear when the thigh is pierced with a skewer.

For the salmoriglio, pound the garlic with a generous pinch of salt to a paste, add the oregano and chop to a paste, then add to a jug/pitcher with the oil, lemon juice and black pepper. Serve with the chicken with lemon wedges for squeezing over.

Gently poaching the chicken and serving it with the wild garlic salsa and thinly sliced radishes results in a delicate dish for a summer meal. If the wild garlic is out of season, you can use a selection of soft green herbs instead. This dish tastes clean and fresh.

Poached chicken breasts
with wild garlic salsa verde

SALSA VERDE
20 g/3/4 oz. wild garlic or 2 garlic cloves, crushed
3 anchovy fillets, finely chopped
15 g/1/2 oz. flat-leaf parsley, coarsely chopped
2 tablespoons small capers in vinegar, rinsed and drained
1 tablespoon white wine vinegar
zest and juice of 1/2 lemon
80 ml/1/3 cup extra virgin olive oil
salt and freshly ground black pepper

POACHED CHICKEN
1 carrot, roughly sliced
1 celery stick/rib, roughly chopped
3 large garlic cloves
1/2 small bunch of flat-leaf parsley
3 lemon rinds
4 skinless boneless chicken breasts

TO SERVE
blanched fresh broad/fava beans
watercress
radish slices

Serves 4

For the salsa verde, blend the garlic leaves or garlic cloves, anchovies, parsley, capers, vinegar and lemon zest and juice to a coarse paste in a food processor. With the motor running, add the olive oil in a thin steady stream, then season to taste. Set aside until ready to use.

For the poached chicken, put the carrot, celery and garlic in a large saucepan. Add the parsley, lemon rinds, salt, chicken breasts, and 1 litre/4 cups cold water (adding a little more water if it doesn't quite cover the chicken). Bring to the boil, then immediately lower to a simmer and cook over a very low heat for 10–12 minutes, or until the juices run clear in the thickest part of the breast.

Remove the pan from the heat and scoop out the chicken breasts from the poaching liquid. Slice or tear the chicken, serve with the broad beans, watercress, radishes and a drizzle of salsa verde.

This simple and very tasty recipe hails from Taormina on the beautiful island of Sicily. Using bay leaves on the skewers really helps to impart the earthy, herby flavours through the dish.

Grilled herb-stuffed pork skewers with bay leaves

100 g/3½ oz. pancetta, smoked or unsmoked, diced
1 garlic clove, crushed
1 UK large/US extra large egg
2 tablespoons chopped flat-leaf parsley
1 thick slice of country-style bread, soaked in warm water for 10 minutes and squeezed dry
750 g/1 lb. 10 oz. pork loin, cut into 12 thin slices
6 x 5-cm/2-in. squares of country bread
about 36 bay leaves
100 ml/7 tablespoons olive oil
salt and freshly ground black pepper

6 skewers

Serves 4–6

Put the pancetta, garlic, egg, parsley, bread and some salt in a bowl and mix well.

Gently beat the pork slices until uniformly thin. Spread each slice with a dollop of the pancetta mixture. Roll into cylinders and tie with kitchen string/twine.

Preheat a grill/broiler or barbecue/outdoor grill and coat the grill rack with oil. Thread each of the skewers with 2 pork bundles separated by bread squares and fresh bay leaves. Arrange the skewers on a baking sheet, drizzle with oil and season well with salt and pepper. Grill/broil over a medium heat for 10–15 minutes, turning so that all sides are cooked evenly. Serve at once.

BAY

Bay leaves, also known as laurel leaves, have a long history. They have been cultivated in the Mediterranean since ancient times for medicinal and culinary uses. In fact, wreaths made from laurel leaves adorned the heads of Emperors in Ancient Rome where they were a symbol of victory.

Elegant but very straightforward, polenta treated well is utterly divine and pairs beautifully with steak.

Steak & polenta chips
with lemon parsley pesto

30 g/1½ tablespoons unsalted butter
100g/⅔ cup quick-cook polenta
zest of 1 lemon
25 g/⅓ cup grated Parmesan cheese
4 x 200 g/7 oz. sirloin steaks,
    1–2-cm/ ½– ¾-in. thick
1 tablespoon groundnut/peanut oil,
    plus extra for deep frying
2 tablespoons 'oo' Italian flour, to coat
1 egg, beaten
40 g/¾ cup panko crumbs
salt and freshly ground black pepper

LEMON PARSLEY PESTO
a handful of rocket/arugula
2 handfuls of flat-leaf parsley
10 g/⅓ oz. pine nuts
10 g/⅛ cup grated Parmesan cheese
2 garlic cloves
zest and juice of 1 unwaxed lemon
4 tablespoons olive oil

Serves 4

First prepare the polenta. Bring 400 ml/1⅔ cups salted water to the boil and add a third of the butter. Slowly add the polenta, stirring continuously. Add the lemon zest. Cover and let rest for 20 minutes. Add another third of the butter, cheese, salt and pepper. Transfer the polenta to a greased baking pan and spread to a thickness of 15 cm/6 inches.

To make the pesto, combine the ingredients in a pestle and mortar or blend in food processor. Season to taste with salt and pepper.

Cut the steak lengthways into four strips and season with salt. Heat a frying pan/skillet over a high heat, add the groundnut oil and the remaining butter, then cook the steaks for 2–3 minutes on each side, depending on the thickness, until brown and medium rare. Rest in a warm place for 8–10 minutes, while you cook the chips/fries.

To make the polenta chips, cut the polenta into small slices, about 2.5 x 10 cm/1 x 4 inches. Put the flour, egg and panko crumbs into three separate bowls ready to coat the chips.

Heat the oil in a deep heavy pan to 200°C/400°F. Dredge the chips in the flour, then dip in the egg and then dip in the panko crumbs.

Deep fry in batches until golden brown, about 2 minutes. Drain on a wire rack with paper towels underneath to catch any excess oil. Serve the steaks with the chips/fries and pesto.

Pea, mint and lamb is a classic combination that works fantastically well in this salad. If fresh peas are in season do make the most of them for best results.

Seared lamb
with pea, mint & radish

2 tablespoons olive oil
2 teaspoons ground cumin
1 teaspoon paprika
350 g/12 oz. lamb steaks, fat trimmed
200 g/7 oz. shelled fresh peas or
   frozen garden peas, defrosted
100 g/3¾ oz. radishes, sliced
   into rounds
large handful of freshly chopped
   mint

3 tablespoons freshly snipped chives
100 g/3¾ oz. rocket/arugula leaves
lemon wedges, to serve

DRESSING
3 tablespoons extra virgin olive oil
juice of 1 small lemon
salt and freshly ground black pepper

Serves 4

Mix the olive oil with the cumin and paprika in a shallow dish. Season with salt and pepper, add the lamb and turn to coat it in the marinade. Leave to marinate for at least 15 minutes.

Cook the peas in boiling water for 1 minute until just tender, then drain, refresh under cold running water and drain again. Put the peas in a mixing bowl and add the sliced radishes.

Mix together the ingredients for the dressing, season and spoon over the peas and radishes. Toss gently until combined. Stir in half of the mint and chives. Arrange the rocket on a serving plate and top with the salad.

Heat a large, ridged griddle pan until very hot. Char-grill the lamb for 2 minutes on each side, or until cooked to your liking. Remove from the pan and leave to rest for 5 minutes. Cut the lamb into diagonal slices and place on top of the salad with any juices on the plate, then arrange the remaining herbs over the top. Serve with lemon wedges.

150 g/scant 1 cup buckwheat, cooked and cooled

400-g/14-oz. can butter/lima beans

200 g/1½ cups broad/fava beans, skins removed

200 g/1½ cups frozen peas, blanched and refreshed

100 g/3½ oz. mixed fine green beans, blanched and refreshed

30 g/¼ cup toasted pumpkin seeds

bunch of flat-leaf parsley, finely chopped

bunch of mint, leaves picked and finely chopped

½ red onion, thinly sliced

30 g/2 tablespoons pickled red chillies/chiles, chopped (optional)

2 tablespoons toasted pine nuts

ROAST GARLIC DRESSING

1 bulb of garlic

60 ml/¼ cup extra-virgin olive oil

zest and juice of 2 lemons

1 teaspoon sumac

GRAINY LAMB MEATBALLS

75 g/scant ½ cup burghul, soaked overnight in water in the fridge

500 g/1 lb. 2 oz. minced/ground lamb

2 garlic cloves, crushed

2 teaspoons paprika

½ teaspoon ground cloves

½ teaspoon ground cinnamon

salt and freshly ground black pepper

vegetable oil, for shallow-frying

TO SERVE

warmed pita breads

sumac, to sprinkle

Serves 4

Using buckwheat in this mixed bean tabbouleh makes it a great gluten-free alternative. This could be a delicious sharing salad with the grainy lamb meatballs, or part of a larger sharing table with the addition of other elements.

Buckwheat tabbouleh with beans & grainy lamb meatballs

Start by making the roast garlic dressing. Preheat the oven to 200°C (400°F) Gas 6. Wrap the garlic tightly in foil, place on a baking sheet and roast for 30–35 minutes until tender and caramelized. When cool enough to handle, squeeze the garlic from their skins into a bowl (discard the skins). Whisk in the oil, lemon juice and zest, and sumac, season to taste and set aside.

To make the meatballs, add the burghul, lamb, garlic, spices and a pinch each of salt and pepper to a food processor and pulse to combine well. With slightly wet hands, shape the lamb mixture into golf ball-sized balls, then massage them a little to create elasticity, and shape into ovals. Refrigerate until required.

Fry the meatballs for 8–10 minutes (in two batches), turning occasionally, until golden and cooked through. Keep warm.

To make the tabbouleh, combine the buckwheat, beans, peas, pumpkin seeds and herbs in a bowl, drizzle with the garlic dressing, season to taste and toss to combine. Scatter the red onion and pine nuts over the top.

Serve the tabbouleh with meatballs and pita breads sprinkled with sumac on the side.

1 butternut squash, peeled, deseeded
and chopped into chunks
1 egg, beaten
250-g/9-oz. tub of ricotta
150 g/generous 1 cup plain/
all-purpose flour
1/2 teaspoon freshly grated nutmeg
20 g/3/4 oz. Parmesan, grated,
plus extra to serve
45 g/3 tablespoons butter
2 tablespoons olive oil
handful of sage leaves
30 g/1 oz. walnuts, chopped
salt and freshly ground black pepper

Serves 2

SAGE

Sage has a long history of use
as both a spice and for health
purposes. It was used as a
herbal remedy in ancient
Greece and Rome, as well as in
Chinese medicine. And as well
as its culinary uses, it can help
to soothe sore throats and
reduce cholesterol levels.

This dish hits the mark when you are looking for something lighter than potato gnocchi but just as comforting. The addition of ricotta, makes a sweet, earthy and creamy dish.

Butternut & ricotta gnocchi with walnuts & sage

Place the squash in a saucepan of boiling water and cook for 15 minutes, then drain well. Transfer to a bowl and mash with a masher or fork. Tip into a sieve/strainer or colander and press with a spoon to squeeze out as much water as possible.

Place the mashed squash in a bowl. Add the egg, along with the ricotta, flour, nutmeg and Parmesan. Season with salt and pepper and stir to mix. You should have a thick, slightly sticky mixture – not quite a dough but close to it. Set aside.

Bring a saucepan of water to the boil. Scoop 1 tablespoon out of the gnocchi mix. Scoop between two spoons to shape into an oval and drop into the water. Repeat until you have 6–8 gnocchi in the pan. Simmer for 2–4 minutes until they float – the water will go cloudy.

Lift the gnocchi out of the pan with a slotted spoon and repeat with the rest of the mix.

Melt half the butter with a splash of oil in a frying pan/skillet over a medium heat. Add the gnocchi and fry for about 5–8 minutes until golden, turning once or twice.

Melt the rest of the butter in the pan. Pick the sage leaves off the stalks and add them to the pan with the walnuts. Fry for 1 minute until they sizzle, then spoon over the gnocchi. Serve with extra Parmesan.

Ideal for gluten-intolerant guests, but don't reserve this dish just for them. It is so, so good. You can be imaginative with your fillings – spinach works brilliantly – and oregano is a welcome addition.

Herby frittata lasagne

8 UK large/US extra large eggs

125 g/2 cups Parmesan cheese, grated, plus extra for the top of the dish

handful of basil, finely chopped

handful of flat-leaf parsley, finely chopped

4 tablespoons olive oil

125 g/4½ oz. passata/strained tomatoes, or good homemade tomato sauce

200 g/9 oz. ricotta salata (pressed, salted, dried and aged ricotta) or buffalo mozzarella, grated

250 g/4½ cups spinach, chopped and stems removed

salt and freshly ground black pepper

Serves 4

Combine the eggs and Parmesan cheese in a bowl, season with salt and pepper and add the basil and parsley.

Heat 1 tablespoon of the oil in a large frying pan/skillet and add 3 tablespoons of the egg mixture. Cook over medium heat for 4 minutes to make a frittata. Flip the frittata and cook the other side until lightly golden on both sides. Remove from the pan and continue until all the oil and egg mixture is used up and you have a stack of frittatas.

Preheat the oven to 200°C (400°F) Gas 6. Grease an ovenproof dish and cut the frittatas into strips.

Place a layer of passata in the dish, then frittata strips, then ricotta or mozzarella and a handful of spinach. Continue in this way, until you have three layers.

Scatter over a thin layer of Parmesan cheese to cover the top. Cover with foil and bake in the preheated oven for about 20 minutes, until bubbling. Serve hot.

This is a super tasty alternative to steak tartare and a great side or appetizer, or serve as canapés for a crowd. It is also nice piled into a bowl with the bread on the side, for people to help themselves.

Aubergine tartare with flat-leaf parsley salad

2 aubergines/eggplants, cut into small cubes
2 tablespoons olive oil, plus extra for brushing
20 thin baguette slices
2 tablespoons finely chopped mixed herbs (chervil, parsley, tarragon)
1 teaspoon cornichons, finely chopped
1 teaspoon capers, finely chopped
1 teaspoon Dijon mustard
juice of 1 lemon
Tabasco sauce and parsley oil, to taste
salt and freshly ground black pepper

PARSLEY SALAD
50 g/1¾ oz. flat-leaf parsley, coarsely torn
15 ml/1 tablespoon extra virgin olive oil
3 spring onions/scallions, thinly sliced
juice of ½ lemon

Serves 4

Preheat the oven to 180°C (350°F) Gas 4. Line a baking sheet with non-stick baking paper.

Place the aubergine in a single layer on the lined baking sheet, season well with salt and pepper and drizzle with olive oil. Bake in the preheated oven for 20–25 minutes until golden brown.

Brush the baguette slices with olive oil, season to taste and bake, turning once, for 5–7 minutes until golden and crisp. Set aside to cool.

For the parsley salad, combine all the ingredients in a bowl, toss lightly to combine and set aside.

Put the roasted aubergine in a large bowl with the remaining ingredients, stir to combine and season to taste. Pile onto the toasted crostini, top with parsley salad (or serve alongside) and enjoy.

FLAT-LEAF PARSLEY

Flat-leaf parsley has a more robust flavour and is lighter in colour than it's curly counterpart. They can be used interchangeably, but the fact that the flat-leaf variety is easier to clean (the curly leaves are magnets for dirt), makes them slightly more popular.

A light summer bowl of pasta, gently braised with broad/fava beans, peas and mint for gentle, delicate flavours. This is easily made into a vegan dish by using vegan cheese.

Braised broad beans & peas
with mint & trofie pasta

1 kg/2¼ lb. broad/fava beans, podded (250 g/9 oz. podded weight)
150 g/5½ oz. frozen garden peas
300 g/10½ oz. trofie pasta
2 tablespoons olive oil
8 thin pancetta slices (optional)
2 garlic cloves, crushed
50 ml/3½ tablespoons white wine
100 ml/generous ⅓ cup vegetable stock
3 tablespoons mint leaves, finely chopped, plus extra to garnish
4 tablespoons grated Parmesan (or a vegan option)
freshly ground black pepper

Serves 4

Cook the broad beans and peas in a large saucepan of boiling salted water for 2–3 minutes until tender. Scoop them into a sieve/strainer with a slotted spoon (reserving the water), then refresh under cold water. Bring the water back to the boil and cook the pasta according to the pack instructions.

Meanwhile, remove and discard the outer skin from the broad beans, and set aside with the peas.

Heat the olive oil in a frying pan/skillet over a medium heat and cook the pancetta slices, if using, for 4–6 minutes until crispy. Transfer to a plate lined with paper towels.

In the same pan, add the garlic and white wine and cook down for a few minutes, then add the vegetable stock and cook for a few more minutes. Add the podded broad beans and peas and cook gently for 1 minute.

Drain the pasta and return to the pan. Tip in the bean mixture and add the mint and half the Parmesan. Break up the pancetta, if using, and toss into the pasta.

Serve in bowls scattered with the remaining Parmesan, a grind of black pepper and some mint leaves to garnish.

SWEET THINGS
& DRINKS

Apple & rosemary fritters

2 eggs

125 ml/½ cup milk

130 g/1 cup self-raising/rising flour

50 g/¼ cup white sugar, plus
   2 tablespoons

½ teaspoon salt

750 ml/3 cups oil for deep-frying

5 Pink Lady or Granny Smith apples,
   cut into discs 1-cm/½-in. thick,
   core removed

3 teaspoons finely chopped rosemary

whipped cream or ice cream, to serve

Serves 4–6

Beat together the eggs and milk. Sift in the flour, 2 tablespoons of the sugar and the salt. Stir until smooth. If you can, let the batter rest for an hour or so, or longer.

Heat the oil to 190°C/375°F in a deep-fat fryer or deep heavy-based pan.

Dip the apple slices in the batter and deep-fry a few at a time, turning once, until puffed and golden. Drain on paper towels.

Whizz the rosemary and remaining sugar together in a blender until the rosemary is blitzed into small pieces and well combined through the sugar.

Dust the fritters with the rosemary sugar and serve with whipped cream or ice cream.

Rosemary and fruit is a joy. Nutmeg is such a warming spice, one that I think works wonderfully with the summery sweet tang of a nectarine.

Baked rosemary & nutmeg nectarines

5 rosemary sprigs

4 ripe nectarines, halved and
   stoned/pitted

¼ whole nutmeg

2 tablespoons soft light brown sugar

a pinch of sea salt

1 tablespoon olive oil

Greek yogurt, porridge or rice pudding,
   to serve

Serves 4

Preheat the oven to 200°C (400°F)Gas 6.

Lay the rosemary sprigs in a small baking dish, and top with the nectarines, cut-side up.

Finely grate a dash of nutmeg over each halve, then sprinkle the sugar on top, followed by a small pinch of sea salt. Drizzle over the olive oil and transfer to the top shelf of the preheated oven. Bake for 25–30 minutes, until lightly coloured and very soft.

Serve with Greek yogurt, porridge or rice pudding. Store any leftovers in an airtight container in the fridge for up to 3 days.

Baked figs in boozy almond liqueur, nestling in luxurious whipped Greek yogurt with mascarpone, drizzled with their own syrupy thyme-infused juices and topped with a few toasted almonds for crunch makes a delightful fresh dessert.

Figs baked in almond liqueur
with yogurt whip & fresh thyme

2 tablespoons flaked/slivered almonds
6 ripe fresh figs
a few thyme sprigs, plus extra leaves
    to decorate
2¹/₂ tablespoons almond-flavoured
    liqueur, such as Amaretto di Saronno
1 tablespoon clear, runny honey
1 tablespoon caster/granulated sugar
a few drops of pure vanilla extract
¹/₂ teaspoon lemon juice
tiny pinch of fine salt
250 g/scant 1¹/₄ cups thick Greek yogurt
100 g/¹/₂ cup mascarpone
1 tablespoon icing/confectioners' sugar

Serves 6

Preheat the oven to 180°C (350°F) Gas 4.

Put the almonds on a dry baking sheet and toast them in the preheated oven for about 5 minutes until just golden. Remove from the oven, tip off the sheet onto a plate and set aside to cool.

Cut each fig in half and arrange them, cut-side up, in an ovenproof baking dish. They should fit quite snugly and not roll around. Break up the sprigs of thyme and tuck them in between the figs.

Put the almond liqueur, honey, sugar, vanilla extract, lemon juice, salt and ¹/₂ tablespoon water in a small bowl and whisk until combined. Drizzle the mixture over the figs and thyme. Transfer to the preheated oven and bake for about 20 minutes, then remove and set aside to cool.

Put the yogurt, mascarpone and icing sugar in a mixing bowl and beat with a wooden spoon until well combined and fluffy in texture – you can add a dash of milk just to loosen the mixture if it's too thick.

Spoon the yogurt whip into bowls and use the back of a large spoon to wipe a dent in it. Arrange the figs in groups in the dent and drizzle the syrupy cooking juices over the top. Scatter over the toasted almonds and some thyme leaves just before serving.

Classic shortrust pastry and crème pâtissière topped with raspberries that are then glazed – nothing looks more elegant. The perfect end to a celebratory summer meal, these look and taste lovely with the addition of tiny sprigs of Greek basil to really elevate this dessert.

Summer raspberry tarts with basil

1 ready rolled sheet of shop-bought sweet shortcrust pastry
100 g/3½ oz. dark/bittersweet chocolate, melted
4 tablespoons raspberry jam/preserve
450 g/1 lb. raspberries
sprigs of Greek basil, to decorate

CRÈME PÂTISSIÈRE
150 ml/²⁄₃ cup whole/full-fat milk
1 teaspoon vanilla paste, or seeds scraped from 1 vanilla pod/bean
25 g/1 oz. caster/superfine sugar
25 g/1 oz. plain/all-purpose flour
1 egg, beaten
75 ml/¹⁄₃ cup double/heavy cream

12-cm/5-in. cookie cutter
6 x 10-cm/4-in. individual tart pans

Makes 6

Use the cookie cutter to cut out 6 circles from the rolled sheet of pastry and use them to line the tart pans.

Preheat the oven to 190°C (375°F) Gas 5.

Line the tart cases with baking paper, fill with baking beans, place on a baking sheet and bake for 10–15 minutes until the edges are starting to brown. Remove the beans and paper, then continue to cook for 5–7 minutes until biscuity. Leave to cool, then remove the tarts from the cases.

Brush the tart cases with melted chocolate, then set aside.

To make the crème pâtissière, put the milk and vanilla in a saucepan set over a medium heat. Heat until just scalding and you are just able to dip your finger in. Put the sugar, flour and egg in a bowl and whisk together. Pour in half the hot milk and whisk until smooth, then pour in the remaining hot milk. Pour the mixture back into the pan and cook over a low heat, stirring all the time, until very thick, about 2–3 minutes. Pour into a bowl, cover with cling film/plastic wrap and chill in the fridge until cold. Once cold, pour in the cream, whisking constantly. Spoon the crème pâtissière into the tart cases and chill in the fridge for about 1 hour until cooled.

To make a glaze, heat the jam in a saucepan with a tablespoon of water and whisk to combine. Strain the liquid through a sieve/strainer into a small bowl. Arrange the raspberries standing upright on the crème pâtissière and brush the glaze over the top. Decorate with sprigs of Greek basil and serve.

This lemon curd is the perfect mix of tart and sweet, elevated beautifully with the aromatic scent of thyme.

Lemon & thyme curd

4 egg yolks
150 g/3/4 cup white/granulated sugar
zest and juice of 4 lemons
5 tablespoons cornflour/cornstarch
30 g/2 tablespoons butter, softened
1 tablespoon thyme leaves, plus extra
  to garnish

Makes 300-ml/1¼ cup

Whisk the egg yolks with the sugar in a bowl and, once combined, fold in the lemon zest and juice.

Combine the cornflour with 3 tablespoons cold water in a bowl, then whisk into the eggs. Whisk in the butter.

Pour the mixture into a pan set over a low heat and add the thyme. Bring to a gentle simmer, whisking continuously. As soon as it starts to bubble and transforms into a nice glossy curd, remove from the heat. Decant into a clean jar, cover and cool before serving.

The crushed dried chamomile in this sumptuous shortbread adds a floral note that works well with the Lemon and Thyme Curd (above).

Chamomile shortbread

120 g/1 stick butter, softened
50 g/1/4 cup caster/granulated sugar
a pinch of salt
50 g/1/2 cup cornflour/cornstarch
150 g/1 generous cup plain/all-purpose
  flour
1 tablespoon finely ground chamomile
  flowers and leaves

Makes 24 fingers

Preheat the oven to 170°C (340°F) Gas 3.

Cream the butter, sugar and salt together in a bowl. Sift the cornflour and flour into the creamed butter mix, along with the chamomile, and beat until combined.

Tip out onto a clean surface and knead together until it forms a dough. Roll out between two sheets of baking parchment until it is about 1 cm/½ inch thick.

Cut the shortbread into fingers about 7.5 x 2.5 cm/ 3 x 1 inches in size and carefully place them on a non-stick baking sheet. Bake for 15 minutes, then remove and place on a wire rack to cool.

This ice-cold granita couldn't be more refreshing.
Serve on a warm summer's day. Best enjoyed al fresco.

Lime & mint granita

150 g/3/4 cup granulated sugar
zest of 2 limes
100 ml/scant ½ cup lime juice
90 g/4½ cups mint leaves
lime slices, to serve

Serves 8

MINT

Mint is a source of menthol,
which is a cooling and relaxing
agent and is useful for relaxing
the muscles in your body.
It is also used to soothe and
relieve problems with digestion,
making a cup of hot
peppermint tea the perfect
after-dinner drink.

Pour 600 ml/2½ cups cold water into a small saucepan, add the sugar and lime zest and bring the mixture to a simmer. Cook, stirring, until the sugar has dissolved.

Add half the mint (there's no need to chop or remove stalks) to the saucepan, then take it off the heat. Cover with a lid and let stand for 10 minutes, then remove the lid and let the mixture cool to room temperature.

Once cool, strain the mixture through a sieve/strainer into a large jug/pitcher, pressing firmly on the mint to extract all the flavour. Stir the lime juice into the mint syrup and then pour into an airtight lidded freezer container.

Place the granita in the freezer, then check it after 1 hour. Once it begins to freeze around the edges, take a fork and stir the mixture, breaking up the frozen parts near the edges into smaller chunks and raking them towards the centre.

Return the container to the freezer, then check the mixture every 30 minutes, stirring each time and breaking up any large chunks into small pieces with a fork, until you have fine crystals of granita. If at any time the granita freezes too hard, simply leave it out at room temperature for a few minutes until it softens enough to be stirred again with a fork, and rake it back into crystals. Then return it to the freezer.

Serve in small glasses decorated with the remaining extra sprigs of mint and lime slices.

This zingy, minty and refreshing sweet treat can work as either
a dessert or frozen cocktail for any summer gatherings.

Rosé, watermelon, lime & mint frosé

1 x 750-ml/25-oz. bottle full-flavoured,
full-bodied, dark-coloured rosé
(a Pinot Noir or Merlot works well)
250 ml/1 cup fresh watermelon juice
60 ml/2 oz. Watermelon & Rosé Syrup
(see below)
45 ml/1½ oz. lime juice
30 ml/1 oz. vodka
5–6 mint leaves, rinsed and patted dry
lime wheel, watermelon balls and
finely pared lime zest, to garnish

WATERMELON & ROSE SYRUP
125 ml/½ cup sweet, fruity rosé wine
(a Californian Zinfandel works well)
125 ml/½ cup fresh watermelon juice
(see below)
250 g/1¼ cups white sugar

Serves 3–4

Note: To make your own watermelon
juice, purée watermelon flesh in a
blender. Strain the liquid through a
fine-mesh sieve/strainer into a jug/
pitcher. Discard the fruit pulp and
any seeds, and reserve the juice.

To make the syrup, bring the rosé, watermelon juice and
sugar to the boil in a pan over a medium heat, whisking
constantly until the sugar dissolves. Turn off the heat and
let cool. Strain into a clean jar. (You can store the syrup in
the fridge for up to 3 weeks.)

Pour the rosé and watermelon juice into a freezerproof
container. Stir to mix, then freeze until solid. Remove from
the freezer and allow it to defrost for about 35–40 minutes,
until you can break it up with a fork but it's still holding
plenty of ice crystals. Scoop into the cup of a blender and
add the watermelon syrup, lime juice, vodka and mint leaves.
Blend for about 30 seconds until pale pink and foamy and
speckled with green mint. Pour into serving glasses, add
a lime wheel and balls of watermelon on a stick and lime
zest to garnish. Serve at once
with straws.

Rosé garden

2 large basil leaves, washed and
   patted dry, plus extra to garnish
60 ml/2 oz. rosé, well chilled (a pale,
   dry Provençal-style is good here)
30 ml/1 oz. St–Germain elderflower
   liqueur
40 ml/1½ oz. lemon juice
1½ teaspoons grenadine

Serves 1

Muddle the basil leaves in a cocktail shaker with a muddler
or the end of a rolling pin. Add 4–5 ice cubes followed by
the wine, St–Germain elderflower liqueur, lemon juice and
grenadine. Shake until chilled, then strain into a small
cocktail coupette or wine glass. Garnish with a basil leaf
and serve at once.

Strawberries and basil are one of nature's little flavour-pairing
miracles, so bringing them together in a glass of rosé fizz that's
already bursting with berry notes is a treat.

B&B

a mix of small strawberries (hulled),
   blackberries, raspberries and
   blueberries
15 ml/½ oz. Basil Syrup (see below)
10 ml/¼ oz. lemon juice
200 ml/¾–1 cup sparkling rosé
   (a Cava Rosado works well here)
basil leaves and berries, to garnish

Serves 1

First pop a berry into each compartment of an ice cube
tray. Top up with filtered water and put in the freezer
until frozen solid. Pour the basil syrup into a large wine
glass. Add the lemon juice and top up with the cava. Add
4–5 berry-filled ice cubes to the glass. Garnish with a
basil sprig and a few fresh berries and serve at once.

Basil Syrup

Combine 250 ml/1 cup water, 225 g/1 cup white sugar and
a large handful of fresh basil leaves in a small saucepan.
Bring to the boil, then remove from the heat and let sit for
about 30 minutes. Strain into a screw-top jar and discard
the leaves. Refrigerate but note that this syrup loses its
colour and turns brown so is best used within 2 days.

This sophisticated cocktail has a moreish sharp and sweet, almost sherbety taste that keeps you hooked until the very last sip.

Index

A
almond liqueur, figs baked
in 115
anchovy butter 80
apple & rosemary fritters 111
aubergine/eggplant tartare
104
avocado, green eggs, spinach
& 67

B
B&B 124
basil 10
basil & coriander dressing
67
basil gremolata 87
basil syrup 124
red mullet in an envelope
80
rosé garden 124
summer raspberry tarts
with basil 116
bay 11
grilled herb-stuffed pork
skewers 92
monkfish & bay leaf
skewers 84
pickled lox 63
beans: buckwheat tabbouleh
with beans & grainy lamb
meatballs 99
three beans with mint &
limes 50
beef: steak & polenta chips 95
Vietnamese-style beef
salad 51
berries: B&B 124
broad/fava beans: braised
broad beans & peas with
mint & trofie pasta 107
buckwheat tabbouleh with
beans & grainy lamb
meatballs 99
chilled broad bean, pea &
mint soup 59
three beans with mint 50

buckwheat tabbouleh 99
bulgur wheat: tomato
tabbouleh 55
butter: anchovy butter 80
garlic & herb butter 43

C
carpaccio, tuna 79
chamomile 12
chamomile shortbread 119
cheese: coriander-feta pesto
72
feta dressing 48
chervil 13
chicken: chicken with
salmoriglio 88
poached chicken breasts
with wild garlic salsa
verde 91
chipotle chilli, Mexican lime,
coriander & 38
chips, polenta 95
chives 14
chive & shallot dressing 40
new potato, radish & chive
salad 48
cod: pan-fried cod fillet with
white polenta & basil
gremolata 87
coriander/cilantro 14
basil & coriander dressing
67
coriander & toasted
sesame dressing 37
coriander-feta pesto 72
Mexican lime, coriander &
chipotle chilli 38
courgettes/zucchini lemon
yogurt soup 60
curd, lemon & thyme 119

D
dill 16
dill & horseradish
dressing 41
dill & orange with walnut
oil dressing 37
fish fillets with a dill crust
83
fishcakes with dill 64

pickled lox 63
dressings: basil & coriander
67
chive & shallot 40
coriander & toasted
sesame 37
dill & horseradish 41
dill & orange with walnut
oil 37
feta 48
garlic & herb butter 43
Greek oregano 39
herb 42, 75
lemon & oregano 42
parsley oil 43
roast garlic 99
drinks 123–4

E
eggs: green eggs, spinach &
avocado 67
herby frittata lasagne 103
elderflower liqueur: rosé
garden 124

F
falafel, grainy 72
fennel 17
three beans with mint &
limes 50
Vietnamese-style beef
salad 51
figs baked in almond liqueur
115
fish: fish fillets with a dill
crust 83
fishcakes with dill 64
see also individual types
of fish
freekeh & herb salad 56
frittata lasagne, herby 103
fritters, apple & rosemary
111
frosé, rosé, watermelon,
lime & mint 123

G
garlic 18
garlic & herb butter 43
roast garlic dressing 99

garlic chives 14
gnocchi, butternut & ricotta
100
grainy falafel 72
granita, lime & mint 120
Greek oregano dressing 39
green eggs, spinach &
avocado 67
gremolata, basil 87

H
herbs: how to grow 30–3
species 10–29
horseradish: dill &
horseradish dressing 41

L
lamb: grainy lamb meatballs
99
seared lamb with pea,
mint & radish 96
lasagne, herby frittata 103
lavender 19
lemon balm 20
lemons: courgette lemon
yogurt soup 60
lemon & oregano dressing
42
lemon & thyme curd 119
lemon & vegetable slaw 84
lemon parsley pesto 95
lemon parsley sauce 79
lemon, tarragon & sardine
pâté 71
lentils: roast squash & lentil
salad 68
limes: lime & mint granita 120
Mexican lime, coriander &
chipotle chilli 38
rosé, watermelon, lime &
mint frosé 123
three beans with mint &
limes 50
lovage 21

M
marjoram 23
meatballs, grainy lamb 99
Mexican lime, coriander &
chipotle chilli 38

mint 22
  braised broad beans &
    peas with mint & trofie
    pasta 107
  buckwheat tabbouleh 99
  chilled broad bean, pea &
    mint soup 59
  lime & mint granita 120
  mint salsa verde 38
  rosé, watermelon, lime &
    mint frosé 123
  seared lamb with pea,
    mint & radish 96
  three beans with mint &
    limes 50
  tomato tabbouleh 55
  Vietnamese-style beef
    salad 51
monkfish & bay leaf skewers
  84

N
nectarines, baked rosemary
  & nutmeg 111

O
olives: parsley & green olive
  sauce 39
oranges: dill & orange with
  walnut oil dressing 37
oregano 23
  chicken with salmoriglio
    88
  Greek oregano dressing 39
  herb dressing 75
  lemon & oregano dressing
    42
  roast squash & lentil salad
    68

P
parsley 24
  buckwheat tabbouleh 99
  flat-leaf parsley salad 104
  lemon parsley pesto 95
  lemon parsley sauce 79
  parsley & green olive
    sauce 39
  parsley oil 43
  omato tabbouleh 55

pasta: braised broad beans
  & peas with mint & trofie
  pasta 107
  herby frittata lasagne 103
pâté, lemon, tarragon &
  sardine 71
peas: braised broad beans &
  peas with mint & trofie
  pasta 107
  chilled broad bean, pea &
    mint soup 59
  seared lamb with pea,
    mint & radish 96
pesto: coriander-feta pesto 72
  lemon parsley pesto 95
  pistachio pesto 44
pickled lox 63
pistachio pesto 44
polenta: pan-fried cod fillet
  with white polenta 87
  polenta chips 95
pork skewers, grilled herb-
  stuffed 92
potatoes: new potato, radish
  & chive salad 48

R
radishes: new potato, radish
  & chive salad 48
  poached chicken breasts
    with wild garlic salsa
    verde & radishes 91
  seared lamb with pea,
    mint & radish 96
raspberry tarts, summer 116
red mullet in an envelope 80
ricotta: butternut & ricotta
  gnocchi 100
rosé: rosé garden 124
  rosé, watermelon, lime &
    mint frosé 123
rosemary 24, 25
  apple & rosemary fritters
    111
  baked rosemary & nutmeg
    nectarines 111
  red mullet in an envelope
    80
  roast squash & lentil salad
    68

S
sage 26
  butternut & ricotta
    gnocchi 100
salads: buckwheat tabbouleh
  99
  flat-leaf parsley salad 104
  freekeh & herb salad 56
  lemon & vegetable slaw
    84
  new potato, radish &
    chive salad 48
  roast squash & lentil salad
    68
  three beans with mint &
    limes 50
  tomato tabbouleh 55
  Vietnamese-style beef
    salad 51
salmon: fish fillets with a dill
  crust 83
  pickled lox 63
salmoriglio, chicken with 88
salsa verde: mint salsa verde
  38
  wild garlic salsa verde 91
sardines: lemon, tarragon &
  sardine pâté 71
sauces: coriander-feta pesto
  72
  lemon parsley pesto 95
  lemon parsley sauce 79
  mint salsa verde 38
  parsley & green olive
    sauce 39
sesame seeds: coriander &
  toasted sesame dressing
  37
shallots: chive & shallot
  dressing 40
shortbread, chamomile 119
skewers: grilled herb-stuffed
  pork skewers 92
  monkfish & bay leaf
    skewers 84
slaw, lemon & vegetable
  84
sorrel 27
soups: chilled broad bean,
  pea & mint soup 59

courgette lemon yogurt
  soup 60
spinach: green eggs, spinach
  & avocado 67
  herby frittata lasagne 103
squash: butternut & ricotta
  gnocchi 100
  squash & lentil salad 68
squid: char-grilled squid
  with herb dressing 75

T
tabbouleh: buckwheat
  tabbouleh 99
  tomato tabbouleh 55
tarragon 28
  courgette lemon yogurt
    soup 60
  lemon, tarragon & sardine
    pâté 71
tartare, aubergine 104
tarts, summer raspberry 116
thyme 29
  figs baked in almond
    liqueur 115
  lemon & thyme curd 119
tomato tabbouleh 55
tuna carpaccio 79

V
vegetables: lemon &
  vegetable slaw 84
Vietnamese-style beef salad
  51

W
walnut oil dressing 37
walnuts, butternut & ricotta
  gnocchi with 100
watermelon juice: rosé,
  watermelon, lime & mint
  frosé 123
wild garlic salsa verde 91

Y
yogurt: courgette lemon
  yogurt soup 60
  figs baked in almond
    liqueur with yogurt
    whip 115

Recipe credits

CAROLINE ARTISS
Green Eggs with Spinach and Avocado
  and Herb Dressing
Lemon, Tarragon and Sardine Pate

JULIA CHARLES
B&B
Rosé Garden
Rose, Watermelon, Lime & Mint Frosé

MEGAN DAVIES
Baked Rosemary and Nutmeg Peaches
Garlic & Herb Butter

URSULA FERRIGNO
Chicken with Salmoriglio
Frittata Lasagna
Grilled Herb-stuffed Pork Skewers
  with Bay Leaves
Lime & Mint Granita
Monkfish & Bay Leaf Skewers
Pickled Lox
Pistachio Pesto
Red Mullet in an Envelope
Steak & Polenta Chips with Lemon
  Parsley Pesto
Three Beans with Mint and Limes
Tuna Carpaccio with Lemon
  Parsley Sauce

NICOLA GRAIMES
Chargrilled Squid with Herb Dressing
New Potato, Radish and Chive Salad
Seared Lamb with Pea, Mint & Radish
Vietnamese-style Beef Salad

TORI HASCHKA
Apple and Rosemary Fritters

KATHY KORDALIS
Aubergine Tartare with Flat-leaf
  Parsley Salad
Braised Broad Beans & Peas with
  Mint & Trofie Pasta
Buckwheat Tabbouleh with Beans
  & Grainy Lamb Meatballs
Butternut and Ricotta Gnocchi with
  Sage Butter
Freekeh & Herb Salad
Grainy Falafel with Coriander-Feta Pesto
Herb Vinaigrette
Lemon & Oregano Dressing
Pan-fried Cod with Polenta & Basil
  Gremolata
Parsley Oil
Poached Chicken Breasts with
  Wild Garlic Salsa Verde
Roast Squash & Lentil Salad
Summer Raspberry Tarts with Basil

JENNY LINFORD
Tomato Tabbouleh

UYEN LUU
Fishcakes with Dill

THEO A. MICHAELS
Lemon & Thyme Curd
Chamomile Shortbread
Figs Baked in Almond Liqueur

HANNAH MILES
Chilled Broad Bean, Pea and Mint
  Soup
Courgette Lemon Yogurt Soup

ORLANDO MURRIN
Fish Fillets with a Dill Crust

LOUISE PICKFORD
Chive & Shallot Dressing
Coriander & Toasted Sesame Dressing
Dill & Horseradish Dressing
Dill & Orange with Walnut Oil
Greek Oregano Dressing
Mexican Lime, Coriander & Chipotle
  Chilli Dressing
Mint Salsa Verde
Parsley & Green Olive Dressing

Photography credits

All photography by Caroline Arber
and William Lingwood, except for:

ED ANDERSON Pages 42, 66, 70
and 71.

JAN BALDWIN Page 62.

PETER CASSIDY Page 54.

TARA FISHER Page 2.

MOWIE KAY Pages 38, 57, 69, 73, 86,
90, 98, 101, 105, 106, 114, 117 and 118.

ERIN KUNKEL Pages 3 and 53.

ALEX LUCK Pages 58, 61, 122, 123
and 125.

DAVID MUNNS Pages 4, 44, 45, 63, 78,
79, 80, 89, 93, 102 and 103.

RITA PLATTS Pages 5, 112 and 113.

WILLIAM REAVELL Pages 39 and 88.

MATT RUSSELL
Pages 1, 49, 52, 55, 74, 75 and 97.

IAN WALLACE
Pages .36, 40 and 41.

ISOBEL WELD Page 110.

CLARE WINFIELD
Pages 6, 37, 50, 65, 82, 85, 94,
96 and 121.